PROLOGUE

I call it the new plague. Almost every day, I hear of someone I know, or a friend of a friend or a neighbor who has been diagnosed with breast cancer.

My story is not the first, I'm sure, to be written by a former cancer patient. But it is my story, and my wish is that it gives hope to a newly diagnosed breast cancer patient. If not hope, well, it should make them laugh, because my warped sense of humor and refusal to let it screw up my life too badly is what got me through.

This book is dedicated to survivors, current patients, future patients, and anyone who has had his or her life touched by any kind of cancer.

I hope I live to see the day when a cure for all cancers is found.

Thanks to all my special girls who got me through this. You know who you are.

I also want to thank Dr. Kaplan, Dr. Beatty, Dr. Isik, Barry and Dr. Dobie for their compassion and expertise, and all the wonderful nurses in my journey who made me feel hopeful as well as making me laugh.

CHAPTER 1

THE DIAGNOSIS

Breast cancer is an all-out assault on a woman's femininity. And if you're a woman who has always taken care of yourself and taken pride in how you look and present yourself, it really sucks.

I have always been a girly-girl. I love pink. I love fashion. I mean, I had go-go boots with yellow lining in the sixth grade! And fishnet stockings!

Maybe I should have paid more attention to a particular event when I was a kid. Maybe these things just can't be controlled.

When I was fourteen, during a regular visit to the family doctor, Dr. Fraser, he found a lump on one of my thyroid glands. It's still a blur to me, but he recommended it come out, and out it came with the right thyroid gland and part of the isthmus that connects the two glands. The tumor was benign, and I do not now—nor have ever needed to—take thyroid medication. I still have the scar, although faded, which at that time I thought was cool.

Was that a sign of things to come? Cancer is not a big factor in my family. My maternal grandmother, whom I never met, died of cervical cancer, but that was it. Both my parents had strokes. Mom had hers in 1985, and it was a doozey. She was never the same again, but she was a fighter and lived for twenty more years. The family thought of mom's life as BS and AS, or: before stroke and after stroke. She could never speak clearly or use her right arm after the stroke.

Pop's wasn't as bad, but he was plagued with a variety of awful stuff. With asthma, diabetes, and a life of being a sedentary businessman, he died eight months after mom—technically of old age, but more than likely because of a broken heart and a body he never took care of. Mom died of heart disease. I have the heart of an athlete. But I always figured I'd have a stroke someday—not cancer.

I don't remember a lot about my childhood, other than high or low points. I had an okay childhood: nothing dreadful; nothing spectacular. But I've always been plagued with insecurities—a lot of it having to do with my relationship with Pop. I never met any of my grandparents. They were all gone—except for my paternal grandfather—by the time I was born. I talked to him on the phone once when I was very little, and he was gone not long after that. He and Pop had a bad relationship. Pop left Glendale, California, in 1938 and headed to Alaska. He never went back. So I didn't have a sweet grandmother or grandfather to learn from or lean on.

I was the last of four girls, and I think he was deeply disappointed that I wasn't the boy he'd long waited for. My next oldest sister, Cheryle, was a tomboy, so she received much more praise from Poppa. I was a pain in the ass, I guess, with all my clothes and makeup. My two oldest sisters are half sisters; they had a different father (whom mom divorced way before I was a glimmer), so Pop raised them. And oh Lord, how we heard him howl (tongue in cheek) about all the money he spent to keep us in "nylon stockings and hairspray!" For the record, I rarely used hairspray. But, that was his sense of humor, and as he got older he came up with some good one—liners. He was an original.

Not having a real connection to my Pop's mind made me feel like I wasn't smart enough; this fueled my insecurities, which led to the importance of my looks—which weren't bad…ever. But I didn't get a lot of dates when I was a tween or teen, because, ironically, I was pretty damn flat chested!

I moved to Seattle September 1, 2009, after thirteen years in Idaho. When my cancer journey began, I changed my blog from "New Girl in Town" to "The Boob Blog."

I left Idaho broken. Moving there in 1996 from my home state of Alaska changed everything. I was married to my one and only husband, Ron, whom I married way too young. He was from Idaho originally, although we met and lived most of our married life in Anchorage. My only son, Taylor, was born in Alaska, as was I. We moved to Idaho when he was five years old—going on six.

In 2002, Ron and I divorced. I will not go into that, only to say: it was bitter, and I'm happy to say we are okay with each other again—for the most part. After selling real estate for twenty years and hating it for the last ten, I went back to school to become a journalist. I should have pursued journalism right after high school, since I was on both my junior high and high school papers and loved it. So at age forty-nine, I finally had a bachelor's degree in communications after getting an associate's degree in journalism. It was a very big deal to me, and I was very proud of myself. I'm pretty sure Pop was proud of me too. I was the only one to finish college—even though it took forever! He was very old by this time, and I remember that he asked me if this was from a real college. It shocked the hell out of him, I guess.

But the great recession came along, and I was laid off at the end of 2008 from the newspaper I'd been with for three years, Taylor graduated from high school, and my boyfriend at the time dumped me—by email no less—so I decided it was time for a change. I packed it up and moved to Seattle, where I knew two people.

But it seemed a logical choice. I am five-and-a-half hours by car from Taylor, and a three-and-a-half-hour direct flight to Anchorage, where I have many dear friends.

Now, I believe it was meant to be so that I would have the excellent health care I needed. Seattle is known for its excellent doctors and cancer facilities in particular.

My blog helped me emotionally to work through the horror of cancer. It was also a way to keep my friends and loved ones informed of my progress without repeating it a thousand times. This is the first entry.

Hippie chick, 1974: the year I graduated from high school.

Blog post: Friday, February 11, 2011
A New and Unwanted Challenge

I feel like a real slacker, since I haven't blogged since last fall. Geez—since then, I've landed myself back in a paying journalism gig: as a reporter for The Mercer Island Reporter, which I love and am so grateful for. So, I'm getting paid to write again—yay!

I am turning to this outlet for personal reasons. I see this as a therapeutic exercise, since I am one of those people that feel compelled to keep my friends and loved ones informed on major events in my life.

Linda Ball: daughter, rock chick, wife, mother, student, real estate broker, journalist, bodybuilder, ballroom dancer, lover, weirdo—these are all parts of my journey. Now, I have a new and very frightening journey ahead of me, which I hope and pray will end with "Linda Ball: cancer survivor."

Yep, folks, I was diagnosed with breast cancer January 26, 2011. Color me shocked. There is no breast cancer in my family—or much cancer to speak of, at that. I'd always figured I'd have a stroke, since everyone in my family (the elders) seems to have stroked out. But no—I have to get a life-threatening disease. For God's sake, I haven't even had the flu for years.

First there was shock. Now I'm easing out of denial into reading up on this horrid disease so I can understand what's happening to me.

Here's what I know. It's a pretty good size tumor in my left breast. I first suspected something around the holidays. I didn't feel it, but I could see it, seriously.

I thought, "WTF." I freaked momentarily and then told myself to calm down and get a mammogram after the holiday. So I did.

Then, they (Swedish Hospital) called me back in for additional views on the left side. "Okay, don't panic," I thought.

After the additional views, suddenly they were suggesting an ultrasound—hmm…okay—then a biopsy. Now, I'm crying. That was January 24th. Two days later, I got the call: that I have cancer.

It's what they call ductal carcinoma in situ, which means it's in the ducts, not the lobes—later it would turn out that I also have lobular cancer—and hasn't spread, so that's the good news. What is worrisome is that I am positive for HER2neu, which means I have too many copies of the HER2neu gene being produced—which makes the cancer cells more aggressive. I'm also positive for estrogen and progesterone receptors, which may mean hormonal therapy once the damn cancer is gone.

I'm being really clinical here, I know. I want to understand this and be prepared. But truthfully, I'm scared shitless. I am not afraid to die, but I'm not ready just yet. And I don't want to be mutilated. I admit it: I'm vain. I've always relied on my femininity when my brain wasn't enough.

The rest of this month will be consumed by numerous consultations with a variety of doctors; plus, I'm getting a second opinion from the Seattle Cancer Care Alliance on Tuesday. These are the folks who are associated with the renowned Fred Hutchinson Cancer Center and the University of Washington. They are reviewing my pathology report now. Then I'll see a medical oncologist and a radiology oncologist this week, too. I will be getting an MRI, PET/CT scan, and bone scan soon. Once I decide between Swedish or SCCA, a treatment plan will be devised. Then, the fun/horror begins. One option is to do chemo first to shrink the tumor so it can be removed without too much harm to the breast—which appeals to me. I also might be able to be part of a clinical trial—which sounds encouraging.

I never thought—not in a million years—that I'd be dealing with this. I have wonderful friends and a wonderful man in my life: Ben (name changed to protect the innocent), who is very concerned about me and has been with me every step of the way so far.

So, this new girl in town—now here for almost a year and a half—is getting to know the side of Seattle I didn't think I'd need: the wonderful health facilities here. I truly believe there was a reason God pointed me here, because this city is very well known for its excellent health facilities.

I will keep this blog updated frequently now so that anyone who cares or is just curious about breast cancer can keep up with my treatment/care. Right now, I feel fine. Ben and I are going skiing next weekend to Whistler, and I'm so excited, because I've never been there! We've had this planned for a couple of months, and I'm so glad I'm not in chemo or anything yet so that this trip didn't get blown. I'm going to ski my ass off, take in the sunshine, and thank God I'm alive.

What I didn't put in the blog was that I was so shocked at first, I couldn't even cry. There was also an insurance issue. My insurance with the company I worked for wasn't due to kick in until March 1, so I was fast-tracked from the Breast, Cervical, and Colon Health program (BCCHP) to the Department of Health and Social Services ASAP. I didn't like the idea of being under what is basically Medicaid, but I didn't have a choice.

I was so impressed with Swedish from the get-go, because they didn't mess around getting me on Medicaid. Ah, but more insurance fun would come later.

After all, this is America: where health care doesn't seem to make any sense.

Before the first blog entry, I sent an e-mail to my best girlfriends. Of course, I called Taylor and select family members first. This is the e-mail sent to my girls, whom I love very, very much. This e-mail was sent out on January 27: the day after my diagnosis.

> Hey ladies: I'm sorry to send out a blanket e-mail to you, but I'm tired of talking about this. I don't know how else to say this but to blurt it out. I have been diagnosed with breast cancer. I just found out yesterday. Yes, I am very scared but hoping it's been caught early enough that this isn't a death sentence. They did a biopsy Monday, and it is what it is.
>
> I don't know much else, so don't ask. I loved the doctor who was with me Monday, Dr. Paula: a very smart and attractive (I'm guessing) Indian lady. I'm in the best possible city for this shit. I'm being treated at Swedish hospital, which is one of the best. Also, the Fred Hutchinson Cancer Center is here; UW and so on.
>
> I'm going on with life as usual, so that means going to work, etc. My next appointment, February 7, is to speak to a surgeon and get an MRI to see if the cancer has spread anywhere else in my body.
>
> This feels like an out-of-body experience for me. I'm still in total shock. There is no breast cancer in my family, but Dr. Paula said cancer is not hereditary. Somehow, it just chose me— must be all my hard livin' (hahaha)!

Fuck cancer.

Okay, my cell phone is out of time until the 7th. I don't need another phone bill like last month. Taylor knows and is extremely worried about me. I told him to just stay calm and be supportive. Maybe he'll appreciate me more now.

Okay. Pray for me even if you don't normally pray. I have a few good prayers working for me now.

CHAPTER 2

FACT FINDING

Blog post: Tuesday, February 15, 2011
A Day at the Seattle Cancer Care Alliance

The Ms. Alaska Physique competition, 1984. I came in sixth out of 16 lightweights.
I was healthy as a horse.

Today was my second-opinion day with the fine folks at the Seattle Cancer Care Alliance. The place has a really good vibe, nice location, and friendly staff. I even ran into an old friend I haven't seen in about twenty years! It was one of my old bodybuilding girls, and I swear she looks exactly the same. She was there for breast issues as well. It was so good to visit with her, and I hope we remain in touch.

This place functions a little differently from Swedish. I met the whole team in one day—which I liked—but it made for a very long day. First, a resident talked to me about my family and my medical history, followed by a brief exam. I swear he looked like he was twenty. So, being me, I asked, and he was thirty-one! He was adorable—and a smart little shit. His mother should be proud!

I met with the surgical team, medical team, and radiology oncologist all together first; then, they took off to discuss my case for an hour while I got some lunch with Ben.

After that, I met with each doc individually. I definitely have some hard choices to make about my treatment and, from now on, which facility to choose to care for me. I will make that decision after the weekend.

Tomorrow, I meet with the medical oncologist from Swedish; then Thursday, with the radiology oncologist from Swedish. Then, I will have heard every body's position. I am not crazy about the idea of radiology. It just makes me uncomfortable thinking of being blasted every day for six weeks with nukes. There is a way I can avoid it, but I'll go into that later.

For now, I feel well and am excited about the upcoming ski trip! I'll have four days to think about how to proceed with my life. I liked what the surgeon said to me today: to just take baby steps…one day at a time. It will drive me crazy to worry about what this is going to look like in three months, six months, or a year. I just have to focus on today.

I remember thinking about this time that all modesty had just gone out the window, as I was groped by nine people in the course of a couple of days—clinically, but still…geez. Everyone had to feel the lump—even the cute resident—which was embarrassing as hell. Running into the gal I knew from my bodybuilding days (which was in the mid-eighties), was pretty surreal. I recognized her immediately but couldn't remember her name; then, her first name came to me. I'm pretty sure she had implants back in the day. I found out later she was okay.

The bodybuilding chapter of my life started in about 1981. Up until then, I had been skinny and weak—and was tired of it. I started to lift and just got hooked. I competed twice in the Alaska State Bodybuilding Championships—which was very hard work. I didn't eat sugar or drink alcohol or coffee for two years. I took it very seriously and became a fixture at smelly old Gold's Gym in Anchorage.

I placed sixth in the lightweights both times—just one place shy of a trophy—so I gave it up as a competitor and started judging, which I did for ten years. I remained natural; there was no way in hell I was going to take anabolic steroids. So, I never got huge, but I was in excellent condition and boy, did I get ripped! I continued to work out with weights until the early nineties. Now I look in the mirror and wonder where that girl went. Once you've reached that point of near physical perfection, you are even harder on yourself as you age. But I learned that muscle has memory—which would prove true and helpful throughout my entire life.

Blog post: Thursday, February 17, 2011
A Few Decisions

After meeting with a medical oncologist and a radiology oncologist at Swedish, I know for certain I'm going with those two. The medical oncologist is the one I'll likely spend the most time with, so it is important to me that I choose someone I feel is not only competent, but one whom I like and who I can sense really cares about my well-being.

This guy, Dr. Kaplan, explained things very clearly—unlike the medical oncologist at SCCA, who I felt was rather brisk. Dr. Kaplan also had on a sweater that had something on it (lunch?) and sort of messy hair, which I found endearing and rather human. The medical oncologist at SCCA was a chick with a unibrow; she was sporting her lab coat and talking to me like she was sure I really didn't know what the hell she was talking about, and she seemed irritated when I asked a question. Screw that. She also had a mustache, which was unnerving to me. Has she not heard of waxing? I'd be staring at the unibrow every time she treated me, wishing I could start plucking.

The radiology oncologist at SCCA was very sweet—an Asian gal—but the dude I saw this morning with Swedish, Dr. Douglas, again explained things much more to my liking, and he had on a whimsical tie with doctor-y stuff on it: like little stethoscopes, etc. Trust me, I am not choosing my health care professionals based on appearance, but I could totally relate to these two men; whereas, the female docs at SCCA—I just didn't feel the love.

Now I have to decide between the surgeon at SCCA and Swedish, who are both very capable guys and have been at it for about thirty years. They know each other, and they know I'm talking to both of them, and they respect each other. They're used to it and have said I have to go with my gut and what feels comfortable for me. But until I know exactly what the surgery is going to involve, I can't decide. I still need the MRI, PET/CT, and brain and bone scans to know exactly what's going on inside this little temple I live in. Time will tell.

Off to Whistler tomorrow! It's supposed to be sunny and thirty to thirty-seven degrees above zero—perfect. I can't wait!

Blog post: Sunday, February 27, 2011
CT Scans Are Scary

Friday was tough. I was really tired, and it was super cold out, and I had to stand outside for forty-five minutes at work, doing our weekly "Island Talk." As a result, I never got warm all day. I had to go to Swedish for my bone scan and CT scan in the afternoon. The bone scan wasn't bad. First, they inject you with some sort of dye so they can see your bones. I kept imagining Wile E Coyote when he'd get zapped, and you'd see his skeleton: that's what I figure the techs see! It took about forty *minutes once in the machine, and I actually fell to sleep, because it's so quiet. I had a really nice technician.*

Then, it was time to head over for the CT at another building on Swedish's massive campus. Lord, first I had to drink not one, but two large containers of this stuff I decided to call "gurp." It tastes like chalk, even though it comes in flavors. Oh my God, I thought that if I had to drink another one of these, I would puke. After the gurp has had time to digest, they come to get you. Then, oh boy, it's time for an IV. This is because once you're in the machine, they shoot iodine through you so your veins show up: Wile E Coyote again. The gurp is to illuminate my organs. So, the nice lady warned me that when the iodine went in, I'd feel like I was having a major hot flash and the sensation that I was going to pee my pants. Right before she injected it, she said, "Here it comes," and holy crap, it was the weirdest, scariest feeling ever. I thought I would burn up, but it goes away in about thirty seconds. Nonetheless, I started to cry and just couldn't shake it for a while. It just scared me.

Later Friday evening, Ben and I were engrossed in a movie, and my phone rang. I chose not to answer until after the movie was over. It was a radiologist at Swedish telling me she looked at my CT, and I had a small stone in my appendix, and if I were having abdominal pain to go to the ER right away. Well, I freaked, because I was having horrid pain, but it was gas from the gurp—not my appendix! I called the doctor, and he said I was probably fine, but radiologists tend to get excited. I am fine: have felt good all weekend.

So, tomorrow is my brain scan. It will be interesting to see if there's anything there (ha-ha!). Seriously, I hope there isn't.

The "stone" in my appendix would later cause me more fun. It was actually what they call a phelghmon (a blockage): in this case, a little chunk of feces—gross, right?

At this point, I was really getting scared and worried. Test after endless test gets old, and I still hadn't been staged and really didn't know if I had a future.

I thought of Taylor and my little precious dog, Abbey, and wondered what they'd do without me.

CHAPTER 3

TESTS, TESTS AND MORE TESTS

Blog post: Sunday, March 6, 2011
Meeting with the Doc Tomorrow

This past week I had four MRIs: brain, chest, breast, and cervical spine. MRIs are no big deal—just noisy—and I suppose if you were claustrophobic, they would be awful. Tomorrow, I meet with the surgical oncologist for the second time to go over all of these many tests I've undertaken. I believe we will then be able to chart a course of action; I hope so. I'm so sick of waiting. I just want to get going on this: to get rid of the cancer.

I am concerned that they want to do yet another ultrasound and perhaps another biopsy on Tuesday. I have to tell myself it's just to be cautious; but nonetheless, it freaks me out.

My strongest emotion right now is fear: fear of the unknown, fear of treatment, and fear of getting rid of it and then having it come back. In the books I've been reading, they tell me these are all valid fears.

I also fear being a bald, tired old freak. God knows I try to take care of myself. I'll follow up here once I know the plan."

By this time, most everyone in my sphere of influence knew what was going on with me. My boss, Mary, was wonderful. In fact, she's the one that insisted I get a mammogram when I mentioned the lump to her one day in her office. I told her I didn't know what to do, because I hadn't been with the company the required ninety days for insurance to kick in. She told me to go through BCCHP, which directed me to Swedish's mobile mammogram "bus." When I was called back for second view, that's when I went to the actual Swedish First Hill facility.

In retrospect, she probably saved my life, because I would have put it off until my insurance kicked in, and it was a fast-growing tumor. Thanks to Obama Care, I didn't get nailed with the "pre-existing condition" bullshit either.

My dearest and closest friends were actually not so close geographically. I'd still only been in Seattle a year and four months and still didn't have any close friends. I did have my boyfriend of two months, Ben. It was terrible timing: to be diagnosed with cancer two months into a relationship. It would later fall apart.

I think what really hurt was the lack of family contact other than my real sister, Cheryle (as opposed to my two half sisters), my dear sweet auntie (mom's little sister, who is in her eighties and in Minneapolis), my favorite uncle in Alaska (in his nineties), and two of my cousins. If my cousin Randy were still alive, he'd have been there for me for certain.

Randy died too young. In 1998, he was shot by a fare as he did his job as a cab driver. This was in Anchorage—the first homicide of 1998. That was an event that shook up my world. I loved him so much, and I miss him every day. Of course, I miss my parents, but Randy was my confidant, my friend, and more like a brother to me.

Pop once told me I'd be lucky to have five friends—true friends—who would stick with me throughout my life. He was pretty much correct. I have a few more, and I thank God for them, because pretty much my whole life, my family sure has been a letdown.

The few exceptions should know who they are. Those who haven't given a rat's ass about me, well, you know who you are too. Family puts the fun into *dysfunctional*, right?

My two older half sisters eventually did contact me, which I greatly appreciated. I had been estranged from one of them for four years, so it was pretty surprising when she called me. We don't talk a lot, but I'm glad she cared. The elder sister, who is a master quilter/embroiderer, sent me a very nice embroidered tea towel with "Sweet Sucess" on it. But I haven't spoken with her. Her husband, my brother-in-law, has his own health issues. It's hard to understand, because I think that if any of my sisters had gotten cancer, I would have called right away. It's sort of a big deal, right?

Blog post: Thursday, March 10, 2011
Cancer is a Full-Time Job

Gads, what a week: Monday I met with Dr. Beatty, officially now, my surgical oncologist. He's fabulous. I've decided to go forward with neoadjuvant therapy, which means: the chemotherapy will come first—before any surgery. I've also decided to participate in the I-Spy-2 protocol: also called a trial or clinical study. I've always felt I haven't done enough for mankind (or in this case, womankind), so if I can help find a cure by being a guinea pig, why not? What it means to me also is that in addition to the standard care, which is top-drawer at Swedish, I get extra attention, because I'm involved in the trial. And get this—I just found this out yesterday from Barry (my new best friend: he's Dr. Kaplan's nurse oncologist and one of the two main coordinators for I-Spy-2 in Seattle)— I'm the first one in Seattle to be chosen for the study! So, I'm sort of a rock star! The reason is because: (1) I have a very large tumor that hasn't spread to other parts of my body and which seemingly came out of nowhere, and (2) my markers (HER2neu positive and ER PR positive) are exactly what they are looking for in a candidate for the study. So, they're all over me like white on rice!

Tuesday was awful: eight hours with doctors and/or techs of some sort. The morning started out at 7:30—with no coffee or food—for the dreaded PET scan. Once again, I had to drink gurp. I hate that shit so badly: gives you gas and makes you poop like a goose all day. The PET is fascinating, however. The machine reads every freaking cell in your body—amazing! Everything is fine; there's no cancer anywhere else. From the PET, I met with Dr. Kaplan, my medical oncologist and the one I love so much. (He's got this whole Marcus Welby, M.D. thing going on: he is so sweet and highly respected; again—rock star). We talked about I-Spy; I met Barry; it's all good. Then I had to go back to First Hill Diagnostics for another ultrasound—this time on my right breast—just to be sure there was absolutely nothing there. Well, there's not, but the breast MRI did find another tiny spot in my left breast: the one with the big tumor. This one is the size of a pea, seriously. So, this absolutely wonderful Dr. Porter did a biopsy on that one. He's internationally known for breast imaging—I'm not kidding. He's another rock star! I watched on the ultrasound screen as he did it. It's kind of creepy but, again, fascinating, because he had to be really precise to get a sample of that dude, and he got it perfectly. It was painless until he had to put a clip in to mark where they took the sample, and that made me cry a little bit.

So, yesterday I saw Barry and Dr. Kaplan again for blood work and yet another biopsy for the I-Spy trial. The trial pays for those, because they are in addition to standard care. This time it was a doctor Parikh who took the samples—five, all told, from the big tumor—and he was great too. I hardly felt a thing. However, from two biopsies in two days, old lefty looks like it's been in a bar fight!

Today and tomorrow I'm off the hook, thank God. I need to get some work done! And my little darling, Taylor, is coming to see me this weekend! He will get to meet Ben—which should be interesting.

Monday, I go back to First Hill Diagnostics for another breast MRI to document the clips, and then I have a MUGA Scan, which will check my heart thoroughly to be sure I'm ready for chemo and then a pre-op regarding insertion of a port for the chemo. It will be under my skin in my upper chest, and they say no one will even know it's there. Beatty will put that in. Then, if all goes as planned, chemo starts March 25. Am I scared? Yes, but I want to kill this son-of-a-bitch.

My chemo will be once a week for twelve weeks. After that, it moves to every three weeks for another twelve weeks. Along the way, there will be numerous tests to see how I'm doing. After chemo—assuming this works and the big tumor shrinks—Dr. Beatty will pluck it out; then, I'll have to undergo radiation to kill any leftover cancer cells.

I will lose my hair; it's a given. It pisses me off, because it looks so pretty now, but I found out yesterday my insurance covers 70 percent of a wig, because it's considered a prosthetic! Yay! One nurse sort *of pissed me off yesterday. I heard that you're not supposed to cut your nails during chemo. Chemo compromises your immune system, so you have to be really careful not to cut yourself or be near sick people. So, I asked her, and she said that wasn't true. So, I asked her if it was okay then to keep getting my nails done while in chemo, and she was real snippy with me, went and asked Dr. Kaplan, and came back and said no. I explained to her that my nails are not acrylic, which I know is toxic; they are gel. She dismissed the conversation as unimportant, and I said, "Look, I'm going to lose my hair; can't I at least have my nails done?" She started blabbing again and I just walked away. Christina, my lovely nail tech, is not going to cut me: she hasn't yet. And I saw her last night, and she does plenty of nails on cancer patients. So fuck the bitchy nurse with dishwater blonde hair and ugly nails! I'm a girly-girl and would like to maintain some dignity throughout this ordeal!*

I did go through this ordeal with as much dignity as I could. As I've said, low self-esteem has been an issue my entire life, and I've always taken pride in how I looked and have kept myself up through exercise, eating as well as I could, and keeping my hair, makeup, and nails kept.

I loved my Pop, but we sure had a rough relationship for many years. It sure didn't help when I was about age twelve (I'm not sure), he told me I'd never amount to anything. I've spent my entire life trying to prove him wrong and make him proud of me, and I continue to do so, even though he's been dead since 2006.

He married my beautiful mother after she already had the older two daughters from her miserable first marriage. My two older half sisters were quite young when Pop started to raise them. Then Mom and Pop had my sister Cheryle and then me. I think being the youngest of four girls he had to put up with, I got the brunt of his disappointment.

It didn't help that my ideology was completely against his either. Where Cheryle was his yes man, I was the rebel. And it just got worse as I got into my teen years. I was awful. Maybe the cancer is punishment for my rebelliousness: the hell I put my parents through.

I wondered and wondered, "What did I do to get this disease? Did I drink too much red wine?" I asked Dr. Beatty. His answer was: "You're female."

However, in doing my own research, a lack of vitamin D seems to contribute to breast cancer. Living in Alaska and now Seattle, and being half Swedish, it's not exactly like I've lived in consistently sunny locations. It is true that women who live in northern locations are more likely to get breast cancer because of lack of vitamin D.

Looking back on this period of enduring endless tests and being run through gobs of machines, being poked at, and having numerous, painful biopsies, it's all kind of a fog. It feels like all of this happened to someone else. It gets that way. It's almost like an out-of-body experience—like a bad LSD flashback! This feeling prevailed for many months, and I still don't fully believe that this happened to me.

CHAPTER 4

TREATMENT BEGINS

Blog post: Wednesday, March 23, 2011
The Flu, Wig Shopping, Etc.

My son came to visit me the weekend before last. It was a wonderful visit, but he didn't feel well when he arrived, and by the time he left, he was all-out sick with the flu. I didn't want him to drive home in that condition, but he insisted he had to get home to his own bed. I rarely get the "crud"—no, I just get something silly like cancer—but by last Wednesday, I thought I was dying. God, what an awful bug: I was laid up for two days. I think it would have been worse had I not had a flu shot, because Taylor was sick much longer.

I was pretty freaked out by the whole thing, because the plan is still moving forward to have my port-catheter put in Friday morning—followed by my first "blast" of chemo. If you're sick, they won't start, and I am ready to get the show on the road. As of today, it sounds like my sweetie has it (the crud, not cancer) now—poor guy.

I see the medical oncologist, Dr. Kaplan, tomorrow, and they will take some blood and make sure I'm okay to go. The port-cath deal is surgery, so they will have to knock me out.

In the meantime, I looked at wigs last weekend and had them order one I liked in a color closer to my own. If I don't like it, I'm not *obligated, which is very cool. The ladies at this place, "Hair Options," are really nice and work with a great deal of cancer patients. It's sort of a bob (like I used to wear my hair)— only a little longer. I may as well have some fun with this!*

I'm more than a little freaked out about the port. I know they said it wouldn't show; my concern is just that I'll have this foreign object in my body. I don't know why, but it totally grosses me out. I can't even imagine having, say, a pacemaker. Oh!—speaking of hearts, mine is super strong. I had a MUGA Scan, which checks your heart to make sure it can handle the chemo, and they said I have the heart of an athlete!

One more thing: I went to a "get started" meeting last night about "The Three Day," a huge fundraiser for the Susan G. Komen Foundation. I didn't realize the scope of the event: it's huge! In addition to walking twenty miles each day over three days, you have to raise at least $2,300. It looks like a lot of fun, but I've decided to do it next year as a survivor, as I just don't think I can handle the additional stress right now of fund raising on top of the job and treatment. I know some women were in the same boat but were going for it anyway. But I know my limits, and being the perfectionist that I am, I'll freak if I don't make the goal. So, I'll wait.

By early 2012, the Susan G. Komen Foundation made a huge political faux-pas, which made me think twice about giving them any money. I'd been trying to send $25 a month. Their decision to cut off funding for Planned Parenthood—which they reversed within a matter of days after huge public backlash—made me very angry.

Planned Parenthood is one of few organizations that provide mammograms for women without insurance. I was one of those women without insurance. I no longer trust Komen, and I will give to the American Cancer Society what I can.

Later I would change my stance and I am once again a huge supporter of the Komen Foundation.

Blog post: Saturday, March 26, 2011
Port Surgery; First Day of Chemo Went Well

I'm okay! It was a long scary day, but I still got a few one-liners in with the docs: I made Dr. Beatty show me his hands—to be sure they weren't shaking before we went into the OR! I crack myself up! Anyway, lots of waiting around, putting on a lovely hospital ensemble, and all of that before I got anywhere near the OR. Ben was with me the whole time until I shuffled into super-sterile land. I didn't get emotional until I lay on the table in there. It's so cold and so bright—lots of nurses bustling around. Then the anesthesiologist started to do his magic, and the last thing I remember is asking them if they watch Grey's Anatomy, and I never got an answer.

It was about a forty-five-minute procedure. When I came around, they transferred me to a different gurney—just like Grey's: they counted, "one...two...three...and wheeled me into another area where I got ice chips, which were a godsend, since I hadn't had anything to eat or drink since Thursday night—by now, it was 2:00 p.m. Then, I went to the official post-op and finally up to the C-Pod where Ben could join me. I had crackers, Jell-O, and coffee, and it seemed like the best thing on earth. Eventually, they got all the IV crap out of me, and I could see the dressing over the port with the tubing hanging out (which isn't there always, but they kept it on, since I was going over to the cancer center for chemo.)

Once I was out of the lovely hospital attire, we went immediately to the cancer center for my chemo. So, it turns out that the study randomizes you to decide if you're getting the new drugs or not, and I'm not! I'm getting the standard treatment: Taxol and Herceptin every week for twelve weeks, then they switch me to A/C for the next twelve weeks, every third week. I'm not upset, but they have to compare the existing system to folks on the new drug to see if there's any difference. I'm still in the study, and they will be watching me like a hawk. They'll do an MRI in three weeks to see if anything is happening (i.e., if the tumor has shrunk) as well as another biopsy, *which I hate. But these are not normally done, so I'm still getting rock star treatment.*

Once in the chemo chair—in a nice private room with TV, etc.— they brought me a complimentary sack lunch with a nice veggie sandwich, an apple, and a cookie. I wolfed it. This first chemo took forever. First, they spent a half hour putting in pre-treatment drugs: anti-nausea, Benadryl in case of an allergic reaction (that made me really woozy—it's not like just taking the pill when it goes right in you), and two others I forgot, with frequent saline flushes. Then came the Taxol, which went in very slowly (over an hour). I got a slight wave of nausea, but it passed quickly. When Dr. Kaplan came, I told him about that, so he prescribed an anti-nausea medicine, but I haven't filled it yet, and I feel fine this morning: just a little sore at the incision spot, but I have pain killers for that.

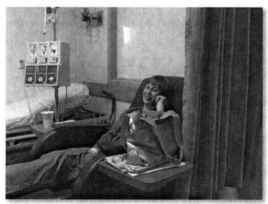

My first chemotherapy infusion, after having surgery to put the port in.
At this point I was in pretty good spirits, but I was also a little dopey.

But Kaplan and Barry (my study group/nurse oncologist guy, whom I adore) said I was doing really well. If I were going to react to the Taxol, it would have happened in the first fifteen minutes. Oh! Dr. Kaplan said not to go and shave my head, because oftentimes, you don't lose your hair until you get to the A/C! But I'm still going to get the wig and some head covers to have on standby. Meantime, Ben went out awhile to go home and let Abbey out to pee and feed her and get himself some food, as it was now seven-ish. He brought me back a cup of chicken noodle soup, which was great.

The Herceptin infusion was a piece of cake: about an hour. There are very few, if any, side effects with Herceptin. After a final saline flush and a change on my dressing, we were out of there at 9:00 p.m.—long, long, day. I was in bed an hour later and slept pretty well. I took a pain killer when I got up, but I really feel pretty darn good this morning—a little shaky.

So, it has begun. Cancer killing is underway! Thank you all for your thoughts and prayers. I love you all.

CHAPTER 5

GETTING INTO A ROUTINE

Blog post: Saturday, April 2, 2011
Progress

I saw my medical oncologist before my second blast of chemo yesterday, and the good news is: the tumor is already shrinking! He said it was remarkable. I've had no really icky side effects—other than fatigue—but I was pretty sore all week from the surgery to put the port in. I hate that that thing is in me. I don't know why, but it totally grosses me out. But, it beats getting stuck by needles every week. The week was a little rough. I was on pain killers for the pain from the incisions, but they made me feel too goofy, so I got off them by Tuesday. They also constipate the hell out of you, which is no fun. I'm tired today—I didn't sleep well, even though they pumped me full of drugs yesterday. My white blood count is down, which is not unusual, so I have to get some shots this coming week to bring it up before next Friday's infusion. The white blood cells boost your ability to fight stuff, so it's important that they don't drop too low. But everything else is cool. I've had very little nausea; in fact, I haven't tossed it once. The fatigue is the most frustrating part. I'm so used to being so independent and just going and going that this sort of kills me. I'm also seeing a psychiatric oncologist—they have everything!—and she told me I have permission to rest and take care of myself and to include some fun in my life: not just have my life consumed with cancer, work, and errands, which is what it feels like. I need to get back to exercising too. That's next week's goal.

Meantime, I am scheduling some fun things. It's obvious I can't leave for a real vacation, but little getaways and events will make me happy. Tonight Ben and I are going on a "date:" dinner at "Dahlia" downtown, followed by the Broadway musical Billy Elliot at the beautiful Paramount theater. I'm very excited, and I'm going to dress up! April sixteenth is Ben's birthday, and I have a reservation at the fabulous Book Bindery restaurant in Fremont. It's fairly new—and spectacular. April twenty-third, we are going to Spokane for one night to see my dear friend Sherry compete in her first fitness competition. She looks amazing. I haven't been to a bodybuilding competition in probably fifteen years. I am really looking forward to this. It's hard, hard work. Ten of us will be cheering her on: all the groovy Spokesman Review gang I worked with. Sadly, only two or three of them still work there. But they were the best, and I'm still very endeared to all those peeps.

Then in May, I'm taking Ben to my fabulous "glamp" site for two nights on San Juan Island. It's so beautiful and relaxing. They are having a half-off special, and since I stayed there before, they sent me an e-mail. Now, Ben's a real camper; he's never been 'glamping,' but I think he'll get a kick out of it. If you're not familiar with my glamping experience, I have an earlier post on it: http://leendainseattle.blogspot. com. I love that place. Oh, and I must mention the coming concert season! Of course, I am still holding tickets for U2 at Qwest Field, now on June 4 after it was cancelled last year due to Bono's back injury. My dearest Colleen will be here from Alaska for the occasion! And just yesterday…drum roll…Ben and I got killer tickets to see my true love Eddie Vedder, solo, July 15, in beautiful Benaroya Hall. I'm so stoked! He's touring behind a solo CD of ukulele songs. I cannot, cannot wait. I keep hoping I'll run into him somewhere, as he lives in West Seattle, and people do see him, but I think he stays under the radar. I'd probably faint. For those of you who, God forbid, do not know who Eddie Vedder is, he's the lead singer for Pearl Jam, the finest rock baritone ever to live, *a fine, fine humanitarian, and a hunk of man. Ben understands. Eddie's married anyway! Sigh. I can still let the music touch my soul. Little things to look forward to make me feel like I can deal.*

By 2012, I'd purchased an ukulele, and I am learning to play it. This is the first instrument I've really tried to learn to play. I honked on a clarinet for a while in Jr. High Band, but that was a hundred years ago. The cancer experience has made me want to try new things and experience life to the fullest, because now I know I can never be sure if I'm going to be here tomorrow. A brush with one's own mortality is a real wake-up call.

It's a fun little instrument: easier to play than a guitar because it's smaller and only has four strings!

Blog post: Sunday, April 10, 2011
More Fun Coming Up

I'm feeling pretty tired today and sort of have the blues, but a couple of nice phone calls have cheered me up. This just gets old: being tired. But I managed to get back onto an exercise regimen of sorts this week and hope to only improve upon it. It makes me feel so much better. The tumor continues to shrink. Dr. Kaplan is thrilled; he says it's really responding to the treatment. I can even tell the tissue is not as dense and hard—thank God. This week is going to be rough. My work schedule is busy, and I have to have another MRI and a dreaded biopsy Thursday (as part of the study). The MRI doesn't bother me at all, but I hate the biopsy. It hurts and leaves my breast all beat up for weeks. I shouldn't complain though. I'm definitely not slipping through the medical cracks. My team is so awesome: from Dr. Kaplan to Barry and Heather, the research nurses, to all the various chemo nurses and volunteers who bring me tea or whatever I need during chemo. They are all angels. My sister Cheryle and her husband, Jerry, will be swinging through this week for an overnight visit. I look forward to seeing her. They flew to Florida from Alaska to pick up a new truck and are road-tripping their way back to Alaska, visiting friends and family along the way. Oh, the shots brought my white blood count up to normal last week. I only have to have one this week. They kind of gross me out, because they have to be given in the belly. I just don't look, and I'm okay. The right side of my chest still looks a little funky from the port being put in, but at least it doesn't hurt so badly anymore. I don't know what else to say right now. I need to lie down. Thanks to all for listening.

Blog post: Monday, April 18, 2011
Chemo Brain

This [chemo brain] is a real term for the forgetfulness and sort of fog your mind goes into with chemotherapy. It has definitely set in. It's very difficult to describe. It's a lot of what we all go through—like: why did I come into this room and to do what?—but worse. There's a disconnect: like your body and mind are on different journeys. So, I've been stricken! But, that and fatigue continue to be my only side effects, so for that, I am grateful; although, they both suck.

I had an MRI last Thursday; it'd been about five weeks since I had one, and even my untrained eye could see the difference from the "before" film. You can actually see the tumor breaking up from this tight mass to now seeing healthy breast tissue infiltrating it. It was great to see tangible results! I also had to have yet another dreaded biopsy, but it seems that with every procedure, it gets easier.

Infusion number four went fine too. I even managed to doze off a little, although sound sleep continues to elude me. However, they gave me some new sleeping pills that seem to be helping—although I feel pretty rough today. Last weekend was great, but I got too tired Sunday. Saturday, I got to nap, then I took Ben out to dinner at the wonderful Book Bindery for his birthday, and we had a lovely time. Sunday I felt good, but my sister and her hubby rolled into town, and I overdid it.

They've been on a road trip, and I was the last stop before they headed up the Alaska Highway. I made a great dinner on my new barbecue, but I wore myself out. I'm still paying for it.

But, I finally broke down and hired a housekeeper—at least this once. They were still there when I left this morning for work; yikes, they were really whaling on the place! So, I can relax tonight!

This coming weekend, Ben and I are going to Spokane for friend Sherry's big show. She is competing in the Empire Classic—in the figure competition. I cannot wait to see the show and all my friends over there. It will be wonderful for me emotionally—just as it was really great to see my sister.

CHAPTER 6

CHEMO BEGINS TO TAKE ITS TOLL ON ME

Blog post: Wednesday, April 27, 2011
Low White Blood Cell Count; Hair Thinning

Last Friday when I went in for chemo, they did blood work first, as usual. No wonder I had been so tired all week—more so than usual. My white blood cell count was really low. They gave me my Herceptin but held back on the Taxol (which is the big gun) so I could get my white count back up. This is not unusual and will not set me back, but it scared me. With such a low white count, the body cannot fight infection, so you're a real target to catch anything. So, I have been very careful to avoid anyone sneezing, coughing, etc.

Last weekend was great—seeing my old pals in Spokane/Coeur d'Alene—but far too quick. I was thrilled with the Empire Classic and how fabulous my friend Sherry looked. It had been too many years since I had gone to a bodybuilding competition, and it brought back a lot of memories. And I got my baby fix: holding and talking to sweet little Quinn, my dear friend Erica's gorgeous little girl. Babies are so therapeutic.

I have visited with the physical therapist, and instead of doing thirty minutes every other day on my elliptical, she wants me to do fifteen minutes every day, so I've been doing that. Sometimes I do twenty minutes, because it's easy for me, but they don't want me to get too worn out. We also added some resistance training this week—weenie weights—but it feels good. Baby steps are necessary so I don't get too tired, but exercise is proven to minimize the fatigue from chemo.

Lastly, yesterday and today I'm noticing hair starting to fall out. I was really upset yesterday morning especially. I know it's inevitable, but it is still shocking. It's not coming out in big gobs—but more than usual. I don't know what to do. I'm supposed to get a haircut Saturday, but if it's going to fall out, maybe I should just have Mallory (my hair stylist) buzz it, and I'll go to the wig. I see my doctor and have chemo tomorrow, so I'll ask him what he thinks, and I will have Mallory sort of examine my scalp and see what she thinks. It's very emotionally taxing.

Chemo princess! I had chemo the day of the royal wedding, and all of the nurses had on crowns or fancy hats, so they gave me a pink tiarra.
They were such angels, always making me smile in the face of how serious their job is.

At this point, I was already thinking about possible reconstructive surgery in case a lumpectomy took a big chunk out of me or if, in the worst-case scenario, I had to have a mastectomy. Dr. Beatty had me speak with one plastic surgeon, which was helpful. Later, I would interview two more plastic surgeons after my unilateral mastectomy.

Blog post: Saturday, May 7, 2011
"I'm So Tired..."

"...I haven't slept a wink; I'm so tired, my mind is on the blink."

That's from the White Album, by the Beatles. Their music always lifts me up when I'm feeling down. When I get to the pearly gates one day, after catching up with Ma and Pa, John and George are next— then Princess Diana.

Okay, I digress. I am sleeping better, but I'm still so damn tired. For those of you who know me well, you know I don't relax easily, and I have a fierce need to be in control of my life. With cancer that control is slipping away. And it's frustrating and, for me, depressing.

I'm doing well as far as the tumor continuing to shrink, and my blood count was awesome yesterday when I went in for treatment. My mind continues to wander with the chemo brain. This is not just like the usual fifty-something "can't-remember-shit" syndrome. It's like having to read press releases sometimes multiple times to comprehend them or walking with a cup to put in the dishwasher, and I'm heading to the bathroom. It drives me nuts.

My hair continues to thin. I did get a haircut last weekend. Mallory did not think it was time for the buzz yet, because it's not coming out in big clumps. But it's still heartbreaking for me.

I'm exercising, but I get hungrier than I used to. Consequently, I've gained about three pounds—great: fat, bald and forgetful.

I had four Alaskans in town last weekend, which was great, but I wore myself out; but it was worth it. I hit the wall Monday though, and I couldn't go to work at all. However, the IT department issued me a laptop (a Mac—yay!), so I can work when I'm not there. Our copy editor, little sweet Becca, told me I'm the first reporter she's seen in her three years with the company to get issued a laptop. So, I was stoked about that. I work on a big iMac at the office, and I swear that one of these days I'm going to break down and get my own for home. I have become convinced that Mac is the way to go.

So, tomorrow is Mother's Day, and my baby is as far away as he's ever been from me: in Texas still, working. I miss him, and I'll probably cry tomorrow over how much I do miss him. My dear aunt Ebba died last week, which stung, but she was almost 93. She had a good life, but now only one of my mother's sisters is alive: Edith, who I am very close to. It's odd and painful losing the elders.

So, yeah, I'm a little depressed, but I guess it's normal given the circumstances.

I don't know if any of you ever read The Shack, but it's about one man's journey to rediscover his faith in God after his young daughter is brutally murdered. It's a beautiful story, which I know a lot of Christians think is a little too off-the-wall, but I loved it, and it meant a lot to me.

Tomorrow night, at the Wa-Mu Theater, Stories from the Shack debuts, and Ben and I are going. He hasn't read the book, and I don't know what he'll think, but I really want to see it. Danny Gokey (who was in the top five on American Idol a couple seasons back) is in it. He's very good. He had lost his young wife—I think, to cancer—just before Idol, and he said this book saved his life. So, it should be very emotional. I'll probably bawl!

Happy Mother's Day to all you fabulous moms who read this. I wish I still had my momma to hold and cry on her shoulder sometimes."

God, I wanted my mom so badly by now. But it's best she isn't here to watch me suffer, because it would break her heart. Ebba's death was a real blow too. The elders are slipping away.

At this point, I could feel my relationship with Ben going sideways. He hated *The Shack*, which wasn't quite what I expected either, but he slept through most of it, which made me feel very uncomfortable. I was also surprised that he wasn't doing more to help me around my place or even visiting when I was having chemo. He went to the first one, and that was it. Poor guy: I mean, the timing of our meeting just stunk. Almost a year later, we had dinner, just as friends, and he told me he was devastated when I was diagnosed. I asked him then why didn't he come to chemo now and then and hold my hand. He said he didn't think I wanted him there. Wow—what a total lack of communication.

Blog post: Sunday, May 15, 2011
Off with the Hair

I've decided it's time. My hair is really thinning, falling into my soup, etc. So, I'm having it buzzed Wednesday. It's just too gross—I want to do this on my own terms. The upside is my legs are staying pretty buff (I don't need to shave as much), and my skin looks great!

I'm not too depressed this week. We had a beautiful sunny day yesterday, which helped every one's attitude. It rained today, but we've got a shot of great weather coming in—just in time for our (Ben and I) big glamping trip this coming weekend! I'm so excited! For those of you not on Facebook who didn't see my link, our exact glampsite is on the cover of this month's Sunset magazine. I couldn't believe it. Tent 355: where I was last time, and I got it again! It's at Lakedale Resort on San Juan Island. I was there last fall and loved it—beautiful island and totally cool setting. I'm so looking forward to it, and we have a whale-watching outing booked.

Meantime, back to cancer—I've been concerned about weight gain: I mean, I've been exercising the best I can and eating a ton of fruit and veggies. Well, guess what I found out Friday at chemo? One of my pre-meds has steroids in it! I have about four pre-meds before the heavy stuff to guard against any bad side effects (such as nausea). The first two times I had chemo, I had to take some steroids orally, but then they stopped that, because I wasn't having any horrible side effects to the Taxol. But then, I discovered there is still some in one of those damn pre-meds. So that explains the weight gain and some pretty goofy mood swings.

Dr. Kaplan has been gone the past two weeks, but he'll be back Friday, and I'm going to request we ramp down the steroids. I mean, I really am tolerating the chemo well. It's just still fatigue and memory that *are causing me problems. But as Ben says, it's not forever. But, it will be a long year, and if I can get rid of the steroids, I think I will feel better.*

Okay, watch Facebook—if you're on it—for upcoming photos of me in my wig or some other groovy head covering! I hope it's a good week for everyone.

The glamping trip turned out to be a disaster. Ben had caught a cold, so he was a total baby all weekend. He was cold, etc.: a whiney, sick male. It really pissed me off, because here I was, the one suffering through chemo, and I kept a good attitude. During the whale-watching excursion, yes, it was bloody cold out, but you really couldn't get a good look at the whales from inside the boat, which is where he stayed. He wouldn't even go out on the little lake in a rowboat with me, because he didn't want to sweat. I was pissed. That little weekend meant a lot to me, and he ruined it—over a fucking head cold. Try cancer, buddy.

The weight gain was becoming a concern for me, too, but dieting is discouraged during cancer treatment. You have to keep your strength up. I was in really good freaking shape going into this: I'd been doing hard-core Pilates and using my elliptical a lot. I always thought: oh, cancer, you get skinny. Not always: between the steroids and my ravenous appetite, I gained ten pounds over the course of the whole ordeal. I'd lost fifteen pounds from the time I had moved to Seattle until this happened. I'm still trying to get the weight back off.

I refused to let the weather or anything get to me, and I enjoyed my glamping experience, even though Ben put a bummer spin on my weekend.

CHAPTER 7

MY APPENDIX DECIDES IT WANTS OUT

also took a few notes in a little pink notebook. On the evening of May 25, I really felt sick. I wrote: "I'm more afraid of living than I am of dying. I feel like my future is doomed to loneliness."

What I didn't realize was that I was very sick.

Blog post: Thursday, May 26, 2011
Bump in the Road

This is unbelievable. Last night I had the worst headache, along with lower abdominal pain. It hurt so badly, I fell to sleep during the American Idol finale! Horrifying! It was pain to the point of waking up with it this morning. I called Dr. Kaplan, and he said, now don't be alarmed, but I want you to go to the ER.

I have appendicitis! I just can't believe this. Back in February when I had my first CT scan, they told me I had a little phelgmon. It's a blockage of fecal matter in the appendix. No biggie:"We'll keep an eye on it," they said. I forgot about it.

It's back, and it's bigger, and it hurts—but not to the point of my appendix bursting and my going septic. So, I'm here, in the hospital, getting antibiotics by IV. I have to stay overnight, and if the pain goes away, we'll just treat this with antibiotics until I'm done with chemo— which is until about the end of August—then, they will have to take the appendix out.They could take it out now, but it'd be risky if there were complications, as it would slow down my cancer treatment, and there would be risk of infection.

Great: lumpectomy and appendectomy to look forward to in the fall.

I'm beginning to wonder if I'm being punished for being such a brat as a teenager. God only knows.

Right now, the worst thing is that I'm starving, and I can't have any solid food. I'd kill for a sandwich.

Other than that, I'm still tired and am beginning to realize I can't do it all anymore.A nurse just came in, though, and was surprised that I was a patient: she thought I was a visitor. I guess it was the lipstick.

The antibiotics didn't work. So, the Friday before Memorial Day weekend, a surgeon, Dr. Florence, was set to take my appendix out. He was able to remove it laparoscopically, so I just have some little scars: the biggest one, above my belly button. It took him awhile to get the bugger out: it was a tough one, he said. He was a good doctor, but he didn't have much personality—not like Beatty and Kaplan. I went home Saturday, and early in the evening, I even went to a barbecue at some friends of Ben's.

Seriously, it was Memorial Day weekend, right? So, a barbecue was a must. But this was the first of several occasions where I knew he wanted to stay and party, but I just couldn't, and I was feeling as though he resented me for it.

Blog post: Friday, June 3, 2011
Back in the Chemo Saddle

I didn't have chemo last week due to the whole appendix fiasco, but I was back in the chair yesterday. My blood is fine; they even checked my iron this time, because I was a bit anemic. I just realized I only have two more treatments on the Taxol/Herceptin, then they will do another breast MRI and a MUGA Scan (checks my heart).

Then, I head into four treatments of the heavier stuff—every other week. It's called A/C (Adriamycin and Cytoxan).

After that, I gear up for my lumpectomy. Oh yay, another surgery! When they wheeled me in for my appendectomy, I felt like an old hat this time. I was petrified when I had the port put in; this time, I was yukking it up with the nurses and anesthesiologist; next thing I know, I'm in post-op and don't know why I'm there! Those were some drugs.

Speaking of which, I got some medical herbs today—if you get what I mean. Nice—and just in time for the U2 concert tonight. Yeah, this old lady will never change. And I'm not calling myself old, but let's just say I've lived some life so far.

Rock and roll—my favorite thing! I bought tickets to see U2 in 2010, but then the show was postponed for almost a year due to Bono hurting his back. I wasn't about to miss this: my first time seeing one of the biggest rock-n-roll bands ever. The staging was so huge they had to have it at Qwest Field, home of the Seattle Seahawks football team, so it was outside. Fortunately, the weather was absolutely beautiful. Colleen and Linell, both of whom I've known since the seventh grade, went with Ben and me. Originally, it was supposed to be Colleen, her brother and his son, and me, but that fell apart.

It was a killer show, but I was only a week out from the appendectomy, and man, I was having a hard time being an enthusiastic rock fan. But I gave it my all.

I wrote on June 7, in my pink book: "The Neupogen got to me today, with the joints aching. I'm so tired and such a wreck. My incision sites from the appendectomy are looking much better. I'm just so tired of the fight. Ben doesn't understand, I know. I'm very confused about how I feel about him right now. It's like we're friends, and that's it."

Blog post: Friday, June 10, 2011
Making Medical History

Yesterday, I had my follow-up with the surgeon (Dr. Florence) who took my appendix out. He looked at all three little incision spots (his handiwork) and said everything looked good. I can get back to doing some core exercises now, although I am still pretty tender down there, which he said is totally normal.

So, I'm in my chemo treatment right now. In my last blog entry, I said I only had two treatments left of the Taxol/Herceptin, but actually, I have two more after this. June 28 I will have the breast MRI and MUGA Scan before beginning phase two of chemo.

So, here's what's funny. I was getting off the elevator on the treatment floor, and I ran into Dr. Beatty, who is the surgeon who put my port in and who will perform the lumpectomy this fall. He gave me a hug, and I asked him if he heard the latest (about the appendectomy). He said he heard about it but didn't realize it was me, and OMG, they discussed me in one of their big surgeons' meetings where they do whatever it is surgeons do: you know, having a pow-wow on all their amazing cases. He said it sounded like a real mother of an appendectomy (he didn't say mother, but it was inferred). What I have learned now from talking to Dr. Florence, Dr. Kaplan and Dr. Beatty, is that I had chronic appendicitis, not acute which is what most people get (where your appendix just decides to blow). Mine was a slow build up, with the blockage, and it was attached to my colon which is not supposed to happen. So I have a whole new respect for Dr. Florence, who I thought was kind of a douche bag because he has no personality, however, he worked on me twice as long as normal to get it out laparoscopically so he wouldn't have to make the big cut and risk infection.

So, I was the talk of the surgeon's powwow, and again, I am convinced I'm in the hands of rock stars.

Speaking of which, if you follow me on Facebook, you will know I was at the U2 concert last Saturday night. It was indeed a beautiful day—the best so far this spring—with Lenny Kravitz kicking off the show. The stage (the claw) was phenomenal: basically an enormous space ship inside Qwest Field.

However, in my weakened state, it took me days to recover. Getting to bed at 1:00 a.m. doesn't work for me anymore. I lay down Sunday afternoon, and I was so tired I couldn't even sleep. Then I got up, ate, got ready for bed, and slept for probably nine hours, and I was still exhausted.

I no longer can party like a rock star, which is distressing for me.

Anyway, I'm okay today, but it's been a tough week. I had to work late Tuesday night and last night, which doesn't help.

I hope to get more rest this weekend. Oh, and my hair is falling out even more. It's getting pretty thin, so I suspect it won't be long until it's all gone.

Just to clarify about the hair: Mallory just cut it super short before. She didn't want to go full buzz at that time. But at this point, it was really getting bad. I would come to where I didn't like wearing the wig at all, because it was hot and uncomfortable. So I wore hats most of the time. I found a few really cute ones, so I rotated them and just wore the wig for special occasions.

CHAPTER 8

THE HARD STUFF

Blog post: Friday, June 17, 2011
Not Much New on the Big C Front

I am in chemo right now—as I was last week when I last posted here. It was a pretty uneventful week: just work and take my pills and sleep; although, yesterday was rough.

They have to give me these shots (Neupogen) to keep my white blood count up. I've been getting them twice a week without too much problem. The one side effect is that you can get a lot of aches and pain in your joints. I've had a little bit of it before, but it was almost debilitating yesterday. I hurt all over. It was a real bummer. I was in bed by 8:40.

Dr. Kaplan said we'll only do one shot next week, on Thursday, the day before my last Taxol/Herceptin infusion.

We talked about what to expect when I switch to A/C (stronger drugs) on July 1. Everyone is different, but he said I might experience more fatigue—great—and nausea. I haven't thrown up once on the Taxol or needed the anti-nausea drugs, thank God. A/C will be every other week, so I will be done with chemo by the end of August—pretty much on schedule. I just hope I don't spend the rest of the summer hugging the big white bowl. I don't know. He thinks I'll endure it pretty well, since I've done so well so far. This whole thing seems to have gone by so fast. It seems like I was just diagnosed—but that was in January. What a way to spend a year.

Oh, it would get worse. A/C, I learned, is also referred to as the "red devil."

Blog post: Friday, June 24, 2011
The Tolerator

That's what one of the nurses called me yesterday, because I've tolerated the Taxol/Herceptin so well. Sounds like a new superhero name. But I'm not a superhero, contrary to popular opinion.

I just met with Dr. Kaplan. Next week I start the new stuff, A/C, and it will be every other week, which is called dense dosing. It used to be they did it every three weeks, but Dr. Kaplan said it works better this way, and they seem to think I can handle it.

This means that unless he decides to go for two more treatments just in case the tumor isn't as shrunk as he'd like it to be, I'll be done with chemo August 12—unbelievable. It's gone so fast, yet it seems like a hundred years ago since my diagnosis.

I was so worried about ending my chemo: for fear I'd never see Dr. Kaplan again. I trust him and love him so much—a respectful love, not romantic, mind you. But he reassured me we're not over.

He told me he is my point man. Even after the lumpectomy (which will be done by Dr. Beatty) and radiation, Dr. Kaplan will be my doctor for a long time: he said until February 3, 2022. I said, "What?" Well, that's when he turns seventy-five and plans to retire. I told him I plan to retire before he does!

So, I feel much better knowing he won't abandon me.

I've been very tired this week and fairly emotional. Anxiety gets to me. I miss Taylor so much too. He's still in Texas, but he'll be back in

Idaho by August, and he says he will come see me. There's nothing like a hug from my boy to make me feel better.

I'm looking forward to next Wednesday evening, as I have tickets to a sold-out Lucinda Williams concert. You either love her or hate her, and I adore her. Many of her songs are sad and lonely—but lovely, nonetheless. Her new CD Blessed, however, is very positive. She's a wonderful songwriter and cool chick. I can't wait.

Blog post: Saturday, July 2, 2011
Another Delay

I've felt pretty crappy all week—very, very tired. Well, no wonder: my white count plummeted again, so I couldn't start the Adriamycin/ Cytoxan (A/C) yesterday as planned. I got a Neupogen shot to bring my counts up and will start next Friday instead. So, now I won't be done with chemo until August 19 at the soonest.

My main problem this week is my right foot, specifically my right big toe. It hurts like a mother. Last fall, the toenail was starting to become ingrown, so I went to a podiatrist, and he whopped a sliver of it off to relieve the pain. It seemed to be doing fine for a while, but then the toenail began lifting and beginning to hurt. I was also worried about catching it on something and it tearing off, which I knew would send me through the roof.

I told Dr. Kaplan, and he had me see a different podiatrist, who agreed it had to come off. So, Wednesday morning, I went in. It's a terribly painful procedure. The worst part is the shot to numb your toe first. You don't even feel the nail removal. But once the anesthetic wore off, I was in excruciating pain. It still hurts.

It's never hurt this bad before when I've had a toenail removed, but this had some sort of "thing," a bump growing up under it—not a new nail pushing it up like I had thought. So, he used silver nitrate to cauterize it—which also hurt like hell. Now it's black and disgusting.

I was in tears yesterday over my blood count, my foot, my brain dead-ness, and everything. Cancer is hell.

I'm taking it pretty easy today. Ben is gone to Montana for a week; he left yesterday. But tomorrow, Jilly and Viv show up! They are my wonderful girls from Bend, Oregon. (Jill and I worked together in real estate in Alaska). I had a connection, so I got us free tickets for a Mariners game tomorrow—vs. the San Diego Padres. We beat them last night 6–0! Go Mariners! So, that will be fun. I haven't been to a game since I moved here.

Jill and Viv are staying through the Fourth of July, and then leaving Tuesday morning when I go back to work.

Work is a whole other issue. I'm really getting stressed out over the whole covering Sammamish thing. I was hired to work for the Mercer Island paper, and now I'm covering local government in Sammamish, too, which is a hard beat. And they want to change the format of the paper: combining it with Issaquah, since they are so close together. I told my boss on Mercer Island, whom I adore, that it's beginning to be too much stress for me. I'm doing the best I can.

I keep telling myself that: I'm doing the best I can.

Blog Post: Sunday, July 10, 2011
So, this is Hell,

I had my first dose of Adriamycin/Cytoxan Friday. This is the last phase of chemo, thank God, because it's kicking me in the ass. I felt okay—just tired Friday night, but I had watery eyes from the Adriamycin. That drug is done with a push, where the nurse (angel) actually sits there and slowly infuses it through my port. It's bright red and makes you pee funny colors for a day or two. It's important to drink a lot of water to flush it out of your bladder.

Cytoxan is a drip like the old stuff. There are many icky side effects from this cocktail, including nausea, which I didn't have at all before, but I've been a little queasy all weekend. However, I haven't thrown up. I'm extremely tired, weepy, and dizzy. I only have to go through this every other week. It's awful. I feel like I just want to die.

Thursday after work, my hairdresser took off what was left of my real hair. We left stubble, so I look like GI Jane. What was left of my real hair looked worse: like a man with male-pattern baldness. It didn't traumatize me as badly as I thought it would; in fact, it feels so much better. I even went to the grocery store with nothing on my head, because I was hot. I figure if anyone says anything nasty, which no one did, I would simply tell them this is not a fashion statement; I'm sick.

I had a wonderful Fourth of July weekend with Jill and Vivian and have yet to post pictures, but I will. Ben got back from his trip to Montana Friday night—just in time to see me all sickly this weekend. But we did manage a little bit of the West Seattle Street Fair late in the afternoon and a bite to eat, which I could hardly eat. He brought me back the most gorgeous pashmina (in purple tones with little sparkles) that looks fabulous with my pretty eggplant sundress I got in Paris. I hardly wear the dress here, because I didn't have a proper wrap for it, and now I do! So, my ensemble for next Friday night's big Eddie Vedder concert is complete—well, except now I want new shoes! What if Eddie sees me, for God's sake!

So, life goes on, but it's hard. I need to go lie down now.

CHAPTER 9

THE END OF THE RELATIONSHIP

I wrote in my pink book on July 13, 2011:

I'm doing the best I can. I am okay on my own. Today, I had to make some decisions. I'm really ill now. This new chemo, A/C, is horrible. Everything, even brushing my teeth, requires great effort. I'm exhausted. I gained and lost ten pounds in the three days after treatment. A bit nauseous—but I haven't lost my cookies yet.

Ben is so sweet, but he is a boy. He never lived through better or worse or had the responsibility of a family. That's the problem. He will always want to run, ride his motorcycle, or now, his new bike. There's no putting the one he is supposed to love, first.

I can't keep up with him—no way. But even when I'm well, I don't think I'll relate to him on a deeper level. I don't know. I really don't know what to do. So, I will ask Dr. Dobie (my shrink—she is a psychiatric oncologist). But I don't know that this is a decision I need to make right now. What I have decided to do is suspend my urge to buy a place right now. I talked to Jeff (my financial advisor) today, and he thinks (like everyone else) that I should just concentrate on getting better.

With the way the economy is, he doesn't see rates going up any time soon, and I am too weak to move anyway. I am seeing nice new neighbors move in, so I'll stay put throughout the winter. I just hope I can get a vacation at the end of the year.

Also, Joni is going to come when I have surgery. Thank God. Jerry had no issue with it and said he'd find her a good air fare. Thank you Jerry and God! I will be so happy to have her here.

Joni and I go back to 1976. We met working as bank tellers at Alaska National Bank of the North, which went belly up a very long time ago. I love her to pieces. She and her sweetie, Jerry, one of the nicest people I know, came to Idaho for Taylor's high school graduation in 2009. No one else came—not blood relations. Joni is one of my sisters, as is Colleen, as far as I'm concerned. I wish I could have had the relationship with one of my sisters that I've had with my girlfriends, but we're all just too different. Joni and I have seen ups and downs in both our lives over the years: some real tough stuff. This has been a hard one for me. But then, so was my divorce, loss of my parents, and the never-ending struggle to make ends meet. Dr. Dobie said I needed more instrumental support from someone: Ben or whoever. What she meant was someone to actually lend me a helping hand with household stuff: maybe cook me a meal. But no one offered. I realized I was on my own with this shit—except for Abbey. She's always there for me, and happy to see me and hang out with me, even when I was too weak to take her for a proper walk. She's my baby: a six-year-old Cavalier King Charles Spaniel. I've had her since she was weaned from her mama. She's my bud.

Blog post: Saturday, July 16, 2011
The Most Wonderful Concert Ever

I don't even know where to start. So, I'm combining last night's Eddie Vedder concert with the latest on my health status.

Beauty first: To say I was blown away last night is an understatement. Here was my favorite (living) male singer in beautiful Benaroya Hall, where no matter where you sit, it's good, and the sound is immaculate everywhere.

The opening act, Glen Hansard, came on right in time. He's an Irishman and totally fabulous. So this morning, I was researching him, and he not only wrote the song "Falling Slowly" but he was in the movie Once, for which it won the Oscar for best original song a couple years ago.

I bring this up, because the high point of the night was when he and Eddie performed the song together with acoustic guitars. My tears just flowed. It's the most beautiful song; it should be criminal. Google it—you'll cry, too.

Eddie's stage set was like a living room: nice rug, trunks, and a reel-to-reel player. The hometown crowd greeted him with ear-splitting applause—great, great crowd. Everything from old PJ fans to kids.

He sauntered out casually and went electric with a song called "Lucky Stars in your Eyes" (I think). That was a surprise to me that he plugged in so early, since this is the tour behind Ukulele songs.

Ah, not to worry. The uke came out next with four in a row from Ukulele Songs: first, "Can't Keep," which opens the CD and is a PJ song, the beautiful "Sleeping by Myself" and equally heartbreaking "Without You," and from 1929, "More than you know." I was mush.

At this point, he visited with us. He said this tour wasn't exactly around the world in eighty days, but nonetheless, thirty days all over the United States, and it was good to be home. In fact, he was so happy to be home, he couldn't wait to do laundry. Wait a minute, he says, yeah, his wife knows "that fucker doesn't do laundry!" He was so funny and sincere. We were all in stitches. There were also ongoing jokes all night *about it being a bad week for male genitalia, what with the lady cutting off her husband's you-know-what and tossing it in the garbage disposal. Eddie said he didn't know if he could do dishes now either, because he can't look at a garbage disposal!*

From 1929, he leaped to sometime in the seventies, performing a lovely Pete Townshend song that Pete did on uke originally, called "I Like Every Minute of the Day." It was so positive and uplifting—just what I need these days.

It surprised me that we were the first audience to hear "Longing to Belong," live—the big hit off Ukulele Songs. Apparently, he needed his cellist, a guy from here, named Chris—stunning.

Eddie plugged in again and did a song that I think is from the Dead Man Walking soundtrack, but he also did two songs from Into the Wild throughout the night, which he scored. The final encore included "Hard Sun," which was unbelievable. He and Hansard did it together and rocked the fucker out: with smoke and the whole rock star scene—first real rock star moment of the night. That is such a cool song too. Read the lyrics online—devastating.

He did a few more PJ songs, including "Around the Bend" and "Betterman" (one of my faves) on the acoustic guitar and a lovely acoustic number called "Rise."

He's funny. He brought out a string section (including PJ drummer Matt Cameron's wife) and said something about not getting boring, and they whaled out "Luken," a totally nutso rocker off No Code, before the totally recognizable and beloved "Just Breathe," and "The End" from Backspacer, PJ's brilliant last studio LP that should have won the Grammy (it was nominated). What's wrong with those idiots?

Lights dimmed: couldn't see Eddie. But then, he went into a very long chant and disappeared—only to come back to don a banjo for an old Cat Stevens song—brilliant! He slipped in the Beatles' "You've Got to Hide your Love Away," which he did for the soundtrack of I am Sam, and the audience totally sang the chorus. He followed with a song called "Fourth of July" by a band he admires called "xx." It was a brilliant song.

Glen Hansard came back out, and here came my other favorite moment. They stood together, center stage, no mics, nothing plugged in, and Eddie had his ukulele. He told us all to be quiet to see if they could pull this off. You could have heard a pin drop. These two men stood side by side, singing "Sleepless Nights," and it was crystal clear. The audience erupted in madness when it was over. I about died.

That was shortly before "Falling Slowly," and I was a happy, emotional wreck. The boys plugged in again for a few more PJ songs, including "Porch," the only song they did off Ten. What a shocker that was! "Hard Sun" was the big encore; they left, and Eddie came back for one more song: the standard, "Dream a Little Dream," off Ukulele Songs.

I had to get this out. I don't think people understand me sometimes—and my love for songs. Music has been a soundtrack for my life. Songs mean things to me. I can honestly say that, other than the Beatles, no musician has touched my heart and soul like Eddie Vedder—and also Pearl Jam. He said he was also glad to be home to get back to "the compound" with the boys and how proud he was to be a member of that band. Pearl Jam will perform live at the end of September in Vancouver, B.C., but they are not playing Seattle. I will be too weak to go up there, I am sure.

So, how am I? It's been a miserable, shitty week. I am so weak it's not funny. Thank God, I only have to get A/C every other week, or I would seriously want to die. I did want to die Monday and Tuesday. You have no idea how hard this is. Everything is a huge effort: brushing my teeth, making my bed —victories. I feel amazingly okay today; in fact, I even plan to go to the Nordstrom sale! But I run out of steam fast. I only worked 21.75 hours this week—a lot of it from home—but I got my stories in.

I keep telling myself: I'm doing the best I can.

Good news: I'm finally getting into a support group at Gilda's Club (named after Gilda Radner). There are only like thirteen Gilda's Clubs nationwide. It's all free, per her instructions before she died. They're really nice, but I had to wait because of demand, and they don't want the groups to be too big. I need to talk to other people experiencing this same thing. You cannot comprehend it if you've not lived it. Also, I never threw up all week! However, my big toe is hurting like hell again, and I'm worried it might be infected. I plan to call my doc when I wrap this up.

Infection is bad news with cancer.

Oh holy cow, I have more good news! My dear, sweet, wonderful Joni is coming to be with me when I have my surgery—which will probably be in mid-September. I can't bear the thought of going through this without an old friend. It's going to be traumatic, I just know. I saw my breast surgeon this week, and he said it's day surgery, but I'll feel like shit for several days. And if I feel less like a woman if they have to take out a big chunk, I'll probably need another woman to cry on.

But last night...that made life worth living again for a few hours.

The next day, I was very lonely and felt horrible—very tired. I knew the relationship with Ben had to end. He's a good man, but I could barely take care of myself much less nurture a relationship. And I wasn't very happy that he didn't appreciate how nice I looked for the concert when it's a major effort. I had on my wig, contact lenses, dress, and new matching shoes, and he pretty much ignored me most of the night, because he'd had a super bad day at work.

I broke up with him over the phone—in a very honest way. I think we are friends again. But at the time, I just didn't feel supported. I needed to devote my time to me. It was interesting, because that same day, I was contacted by my ex-boyfriend in Spokane, asking if I'd have lunch when he came over with his daughter to help her find an apartment, since she was going to be attending the University of Washington.

He was genuinely concerned; his mother died of breast cancer. We did indeed have a nice lunch, and it wasn't weird or anything. I'm happy I can be friends with my ex-husband and ex-boyfriends now. It makes life easier.

It's a shame that Ben and I had only known each other two months when I was diagnosed. Maybe it would have worked if we'd had a more solid foundation.

CHAPTER 10

LONELY AND SICK

C hemo—you don't know anymore what's happening to you. Suddenly, you are just a vacant shell of who or what you once were. It's weird, but you look in the mirror and see a total stranger.

Blog post: Saturday, July 23, 2011
I Guess This is the "Worse before It Gets Better"

Sleep is elusive these first few days after A/C. It's 7:42 a.m., and I need more sleep, but I can't. I went to bed after watching the movie Once at 10:00 p.m. That's the movie with Glen Hansard, who opened and played with Eddie last weekend—a very sweet story, filled with music; I loved it.

Looking back on the week: I had a follow-up with the podiatrist on my right foot, which has been hurting like hell. I called Dr. Kaplan over last weekend and told him I thought it was infected, so now I'm on antibiotics for it. My medicine cabinet floweth over now. I get confused on when to take what. I already had an appointment with the podiatrist Monday morning, and yeah, it should be drying up faster, so I'm back soaking it in epsom salt every night, and it does seem to be improving; although, it will be a year before a complete healthy toenail grows back—along with my hair.

I must say, for the fatigue level I'm experiencing, I did a kick-ass job of covering the conclusion of the Sammamish shoreline master program. There was a three-hour meeting at their city hall Monday night—grueling. I came home and took a nap first and got a great story. Every single body of water in Washington must develop a new plan every seven years, so they are all scrambling. It's a fascinating topic to me, because it totally affects private property rights on lakes, rivers, and the Sound. It harkens back to my old real estate days; plus, the folks up in Sammamish are pretty, shall we say, spirited? Good people, though.

Back to cancer: I attended my first support group at Gilda's Club. It was good. I can't say much, because it's all confidential, but one very smart, pragmatic lady has stage four breast cancer, and now they've found a spot on her liver. She has two small children. She empathized with the fact that I'm on Adryamicin—she's the one who said it's nickname is the red devil: fitting. I hate this fucking disease. She really doesn't know what her future holds. It scared me, and when I went into treatment this week, I told Dr. Kaplan her story, and he said I'm going to be fine. They see no evidence of the cancer tripping along somewhere else in my body. But you see, that's the biggest fear once this is over. What if it comes back? I don't know if I have it in me to fight again.

My son Taylor headed home to Idaho from Texas yesterday, as he finished his summer job there. Once he gets settled back at his dad's, he'll come see me. I'm so proud of him for sticking it out in that heat. And he has grown up so much; I can tell. He's going to go back into the firefighting school in the fall—which he started after high school but didn't finish. His first semester will be EMT I stuff. It's a perfect career for him. He's strong, brave, and handsome! So, he could be on one of those shirtless firefighter calendars. (I told him this before, and he cringed)!

It's a beautiful day, and I hope to be strong enough to take Abbey down to Alki for the open-air art fair. We'll have to go after her grooming, of course, so she looks pretty! Hell, she looks better than I do.

I was lonely, yet I wanted to be left alone; this was how I felt a lot of the time. No one can understand this until it happens to them. The emotional roller coaster was mainly due to the steroids to counteract any weird side effects from the chemo. But it made me gain weight and not recognize myself: not just physically, but mentally.

Blog post: Saturday, July 30, 2011
An Angel on a Street Corner; Debt Crisis Freaking Me Out

I love the weekends when I haven't just had chemo. This was an off week, thank God, because if I had to do this round every week—well, I don't think I could. It hit me pretty hard Monday: I stayed home all day and could barely function. But I made it to work the rest of the week but still only got in twenty-five hours. Again, thank God for insurance, because these short hours mean short paychecks too. And this fight in Washington D.C., which I'm following very closely, is making me very nervous. I don't want to end up an indigent old woman. My financial advisor tells me to stay the course, which I will, but those boneheads had better reach an agreement before the deadline or the sovereign United States as we know it will be in deep shit—i.e., double-dip recession. My psychiatric oncologist tells me I worry too much about things I can't control, which is true, but I need to stop, because it does affect my health. I'm trying.

So Tuesday night, I went back to my support group at Gilda's Club. I was standing at the corner waiting to cross Broadway to Gilda's, and this blond angel came up beside me and said, "I'm a one-year survivor." I looked at her, sort of shocked, and said, "How did you know?"

She said she just could tell and figured I was headed to Gilda's. She said, "It gets better; I want you to know that." She hugged me, and I started to cry. We talked through another light, and I asked her how old she was, because she didn't look very old. She's only thirty-seven, blond, and pretty, and she told me she just had her last reconstructive surgery and sort of perked her boobs up. She gave me her business card and told me to e-mail or call anytime, and she'd be there for me. I have e-mailed her but haven't heard back, but I was blown away—an angel.

Then at group, the one same lady was there from last week, and she does indeed have a tumor on her liver now. It's not good. A fellow I hadn't met was there, and he has some sort of cancer in the bone marrow that is not curable but is treatable. So, he's on chemo (pills) the rest of his life. I hate this disease so much. But the group was good. We laughed and cried, and they were amazed by my encounter on the street.

So, get this: Some scumbag from hell sawed all the copper pipes off the back of Gilda's Club, so now they have no heat or A/C. I asked Marti, our facilitator, why someone would do that, and she said they sell the copper for drug money. Can you imagine—doing that to a nonprofit? It made the news, as they had a camp for kids with cancer there all week during the day, and they were sweltering but still had fun. They need ten thousand dollars to fix it. I plan to give what I can next time I'm there. It's just tragic.

By Thursday, one week since my last chemo, I began to feel human again. So, I'll have a good week this week until Friday when they hit me again. But then, I'll only have one left!

Taylor got back to Idaho in one piece last Sunday. He's going to the Gorge tonight to see Soundgarden. I'm so jealous. This will be the first summer since I moved to the "lower 48" in 1996 that I haven't gone to the Gorge. I just don't have the energy. It's a lot of work: with the traffic, accommodations, walking, etc. I told him I've heard rumors that one of the Pearl Jam guys might pop up on stage. Taylor's never understood my obsession with PJ, but I gave him the lecture that they've been together now for twenty years, so they've proven they are not just a flash-in-the-pan grunge group, which seems funny to think now. He said one of his buddies that is going will freak if a PJ member shows up, because he loves them too.

Speaking of which…when I saw Eddie Vedder at Benaroya Hall, I could not get my hands on one of these very cool posters by a local artist called Munk One, as they sold out. Well, through the Internet and perseverance, I got one! It turns out a guy who lives right here in West Seattle bought an extra one, so I paid him sixty dollars for it—they were thirty-five dollars at the show but are going for much higher now on ebay. I'll try to find a link to it to post to FB. Anyway, when I went to the Alki Arts Fair last weekend, I found this fellow, Fred, who does custom matting and framing. I met him when I was first here in

Seattle—through a little coffee group I got into, which has since broken apart. I went to his studio Wednesday with the poster, and it's going to be flat out fantastic once it's matted and framed. He and his wife live off California Avenue, a main north/south in West Seattle. So, he asked me if I know who Chris Cornell is, and I said, yes, of course (lead singer for Soundgarden). Well, he used to live four houses down from Fred, and now his ex-wife lives there. Cornell's ex-wife is Susan Silver, who was a huge influence in the nineties music scene in Seattle. I think at one time, she managed Alice in Chains. Anyway, so I asked Fred if he's ever run into Vedder, and he said he's seen him around—he just lives off California a few blocks up, he said. So, what I'm getting to, is that the house I've been driving people by when they come to visit, which I thought was Eddie's house—isn't! Shit! I feel like an ass now. There goes my Linda Ball West Seattle tour highlight!

I've decided to stay put in this apartment—which I've been in now for almost two years—until at least next summer. The economy is too fragile—as am I—to move. So, in addition to my new art, I've got a couple of nice runners on order for my halls, through my interior design genius, Colleen, and I'm going to have my local interior design connection, Rebecca, paint my bedroom—just a few little things to brighten the place up and make my environment feel better, because this cancer treatment will go on and on still. I have surgery then six weeks of radiation ahead of me yet.

On a sad note, but it's of my doing, I am on my own again. It's complicated and personal, but if anyone is reading this who knows Ben, I want to say that he is a kind, sweet man. This is about me. I can hardly take care of myself sometimes, and it's even harder to nurture a relationship. I just can't do it right now. I'm sorry. Chalk it up to another failed relationship.

Out of respect for Ben, I didn't report the break-up on my blog for a couple of weeks. With regard to my support group, I will refer to the lady with the spot on her liver now as Clarice. I would grow very fond of her, and she was really the only one I related to in group, because she also had breast cancer. She was very, very smart and kind. She didn't make it—but more on that later. People really do die from this shit.

Blog post: Monday, August 8, 2011
Madness

What—somebody please tell me—is going on in this world? I cried through the first twenty minutes of the news tonight. A six-hundred-point drop in the market; thirty-one dead troops in Afghanistan—the most in one day in this stupid 10-year war. Riots in London and cancer care providers running out of oncology medicines—and it could get worse?

It's hard not to be depressed right now.

Thankfully, for many reasons, I have only one chemotherapy treatment left. So hopefully, Swedish won't run out of my poison before then, which is August 19. I had chemo Friday, and today (day three) is always when I hit the wall. I feel terrible; everything is so difficult; and I cry a lot.

So, I'll be glad when chemo is over. Next step: see my surgeon August 22 and schedule the lumpectomy. I'll go through another round of blood work, MRI, and God knows what else.

My timing always seems to be off. Yesterday, before the stock market crash today, I booked a trip to Kauai for Taylor, myself, and I think his girlfriend Jamie is coming too, which is great, because I really like her.

But I got a good deal. It's only five days, but it was a Living Social coupon for a brand new resort on Poipu beach, which is where I wanted. Gads, it's a two-bedroom, partial ocean view, with a full kitchen and lanai. And it's a full-service resort with housekeeping, concierge, etc. We get a discount at their market and scuba diving or snorkeling for two, which I'll give to the kids. I'd rather do a river kayak adventure.

So, I'm trying not to beat myself up over this—quality of life is important too. I had to work this around blackout days at the resort and Taylor's school schedule, so we aren't going at Christmas, which would have been great, but who seriously can afford that? So, we're going December 10–15, and I look at it as hopefully my "I survived" journey.

Meantime, I worry…about everything. Please, someone, tell me things are going to get better.

I am happy with Seattle. When the weather is nice here—which it has been lately—it's so beautiful. I was just thinking yesterday how glad I was to have moved here. I renewed my lease until the end of next June, because I really can't find anything better where I can have Abbey. They treat me well, so it's okay.

Oh, and to top off all the rotten news, next season is the end for Desperate Housewives! That bites! Oh well, I thought I'd be lost when the original Melrose Place was cancelled, so I guess I'll live through this one.

I do hope Taylor comes to see me soon, as I still haven't seen him since he got back from Texas. I haven't seen him since April, and I miss him so much. He is allegedly coming Labor Day weekend—after chemo and before surgery, which is what I want, because I don't want him to see me miserable.

I tried really hard to protect Taylor from knowing how miserable I was. I don't think he fully understood how hard this is on one's mind and body. But I do know he loves me and doesn't want to lose me. When I first told him of my diagnosis, he later sent me a text message that said something to the effect of "get rid of that." That was always the goal.

CHAPTER 11

GETTING READY FOR THE LUMPECTOMY

Blog post: Monday, August 22, 2011
Chemo Over; Surgery Scheduled

I'm still reeling from Friday's chemo, but it's over! For my heartfelt gratitude to my wonderful oncology nurses, I brought them a huge spray of flowers Friday and a long, handwritten card expressing my feelings for how wonderful they've been, but I said, "I'm ready to blow this pop stand!" I got lots of hugs in return and a lovely, handmade card from my favorite nurse, Sarah, whom I told I wished she were my daughter, and that her parents should be very proud of her.

While I'm on the subject of flowers, Saturday I got my five-dollar roses at West Seattle Produce to cheer the place up. So then, my monthly housekeeper shows up with a dozen roses from

Safeway for me—so sweet! So, I'm arranging all these roses, and then, there's a guy at the door with a floral delivery from my friend Barrie up in Alaska, congratulating me on my last chemo! I said to Celia, the housekeeper (I adore her), "It looks like someone died now!" Seriously, I loved it; thank you so much, Bear. They are fabulous!

So, here's the scoop: My surgery is September 14. One of my other angels, Joni, flies in (from Tucson) the evening of the twelfth and will be here until the eighteenth to get me through it. Dr. Beatty (my surgeon) was amazed at the reduction in the mass. I'll have an MRI September 6, along with blood work and another MUGA Scan (checking my heart again to make sure it's strong enough for surgery, which I'm sure it will be).

The MRI will tell the whole story, but Dr. Beatty is feeling pretty confident he'll get a clean margin and even do a little "lifting" while I'm out, so hopefully I won't be too funky looking. I forgot to ask if he could do a little liposuction under my arms while he's in there! Alas, he doesn't do that anyway! My lower body has kept strong, because I use my elliptical and walk, but I need to get rid of the wingspan under my arms when I'm strong enough.

The first step on the fourteenth is to inject dye under my left arm, so they can locate and remove the sentinel node. A pathologist will be on hand. If it looks bad, he'll examine it right away (while they are in there), but if it doesn't look suspicious, they'll have a report in a couple of days. I pray that's the case, and cancer hasn't slipped into any of my lymph nodes. So, this could go pretty well.

Meantime, I went to a wonderful seminar last Thursday night on nutrition during and after cancer, and I left feeling pretty good about how I've been taking care of myself nutritionally. I'm already doing a lot of things right, but I need to eat about a cup-and-a-half more of veggies each day. I do well with fruit, eat low dairy, I'm down to 2 cups of coffee a day, and I haven't had a drink in a while—I have no desire. But when I do, I'm limiting it to two glasses. I could live to be…well, who knows; it's not important. But I'm not ready to check out just yet.

Taylor and Jamie are coming for Labor Day weekend! Yay! I bought tickets for Bumbershoot on Sunday of that weekend, so that *will be fun. I'm excited about seeing Leon Russell! Remember him— session man for the Beatles, especially George? (Leon played the concert for Bangladesh and brought the house down with his own take on 'Jumpin' Jack Flash). But if Taylor and Jamie don't want to see an old fart, there will be a super-hot Seattle rapper on another stage nearby! Leon will probably finish before the rapper, so I'll sneak in there too.*

Yesterday, my curiosity got to me, and I felt okay, so I went to Hempfest! Wow—this is the biggest festival of its type anywhere! This is an interesting city I live in—love it. It was hot out, and I can't take too much sun, but I saw: all kinds of product made from hemp, head-shop-type booths, politicians with booths who support legalization of marijuana, voter registration, bands, old-white stoners, young black and proud, and little adorable couples and families—all at Hempfest. I treated myself to a delicious Hemp ice cream sandwich—all natural, no soy, no dairy, and served to me by a little old lady.

But then the bummer was that I got too hot and too tired and couldn't remember where I parked. I wandered, started to cry, but eventually found it and went home to take a shower. It was such a beautiful day until then. I just got panicky. But soon, when all the poison has worked its way through my body, I'll think clearly again.

I have goals. I want to be a grandmother someday. And I still believe in love.

Blog post: Friday, September 9, 2011
I'm Doing the Best I Can

I keep telling myself that, but I can't seem to get enough done (in my opinion). The last two days have been hard. It's been two weeks since my last chemo, and I was thinking it was three. I can't even keep track of time. But I do feel better in that sense: I don't have the icky dry mouth and sick feeling anymore.

That said, I've been crying on and off for two days. I'm scared about the surgery, which is this coming Wednesday. I'm not worried about my surgeon, he's fabulous, or about not waking up; rather, I'm worried about how it's all going to turn out.

I had an MRI Tuesday, and it says: "there has been a further decrease in the volume, size, peak enhancement, and kinetic profile of the abnormality centered at eleven o'clock,"...etc," Then, at the end, it says, "no adenopathy is visible," which means no signs of cancer in my lymph nodes, which is really good news. But it goes on to say that the "abnormality" had a substantial but incomplete response to therapy.

So, here I worry and worry about becoming a deformed person. And I cry and wonder what the next steps will be. I will refuse to do anymore chemo. I don't care. It's too hard.

So, big fun tomorrow as I go in search of a very supportive sport bra that I will have to wear 24-7 for a few days while I heal.

I am so grateful Joni is coming. I just couldn't do this one on my own. The night before my surgery, we're going to have dinner at my favorite (well one of my favorites) restaurant, Book Bindery, in Fremont. It's so killer—a food writer turned me on to the place. It's only been open since last fall, but it's been "discovered." so you have to have a reservation. Hopefully, it won't be my last meal.

I've been working really hard trying to get in more hours at work, and it was a busy week—wore me out. I worked late three nights with meetings, then a guy was electrocuted on the Island, and a truck plowed into an old woman's house; breaking news is not real common on Mercer Island, and I'm it to respond.

My son Taylor and his girl Jamie were indeed here for Labor Day Weekend. My God, it was so good to hug him. He hugged me harder this time and didn't let go. I know he's worried about me. But we had fun: ate out one night and then drove by the house Kurt Cobain died in—I'd never even seen it before! I know—macabre.

We did Pike Place Market with a zillion other people Saturday, but it was such a beautiful day, and all the flowers were overwhelmingly lovely.

With my son, Taylor, and my dog, Abbey, at Lincoln Park on a beautiful Labor Day weekend. I'm bald under the hat.

Sunday, we went to Bumbershoot, and it was another sunny, gorgeous day. It was actually too hot for me. I get warm quickly and can't take too much. The first thing I did was listen to a talk given by Pamela DesBarres, aka "Miss Pamela," the world's most famous groupie and author of several books: the first one being, I'm With The Band. I read the book about eight months ago and loved every word. She is a hoot and still quite attractive in an old hippie sort of groove. In fact, she's coming out with her own clothing line next spring: called Groupie Couture—can't wait! Anyway, she autographed my book, and I bought the sequel: called Take another Little Piece of my Heart. It was very cool. I asked her if she was the inspiration for the character "Penny Lane" in the movie Almost Famous, and she said she and two other groupies were. She also thinks the Stones will tour once more—nice.

Later, I saw Leon Russell while the kids went to see the rapper. Leon made me very happy. He did a lot of his great old blues but also a couple of Beatles and Stones songs. He's played with them all. I was thrilled that he did his very famous take on 'Jumpin' Jack Flash. He's still got a huge mane of white hair and beard—all under a white *cowboy hat. Love the guy—geez he's in his seventies now and can still rock it.*

On Labor Day, all three of us took Abbey to the park for a walk, and then they had to go back to Idaho. Jamie had a class Tuesday morning, and Taylor started Wednesday. They are both at North Idaho College.

Okay, I feel better.

Whatever it is you do—pray, meditate, chant—send it my way Wednesday, because I'm scared shitless.

I had so many books to read, but I did eventually read Pamela Des Barres's second book. She is such an inspiration. Her experience raising her son was not in the same circumstances as raising my Taylor, but I could relate to the protective mother part, and I wondered if I smothered and enabled Taylor too much. I'm not doing that now—we're miles apart—but I recognize my shortcomings as a mother. It's the hardest job in the world: as any parent can tell you.

CHAPTER 12

THE LUMPECTOMY

Blog post: Wednesday, September 21, 2011
Cancer Has Its Own Agenda—This Isn't Over

I decided to wait until I saw my medical oncologist today to report the latest. As many of you know, I had my lumpectomy one week ago today. I did a quick Facebook post that day: that it seemed to go well. Dr. Beatty, my surgeon, removed 7.7 centimeters of mass, and there is no cancer in my lymph nodes, which is excellent news.

But I am not cancer free. Dr. Beatty called me late Friday when the pathology report came in. I had dozed off, and Joni was napping too. I did know there was another little tumor in another part of the breast, and it was, and still is, benign. However, there is lobular cancer, the second most prevalent of breast cancers (behind DCIS, which I had in the tumor) still in the breast.

I asked Dr. Kaplan today why this wasn't picked up by an MRI. It's not like a tumor or mass; rather, it sort of fingers out in the ducts and is only picked up by pathology.

You can imagine that I was devastated when Dr. Beatty called me Friday. I tried all weekend to process the fact that the plan didn't work, and I will have to have a mastectomy in two to three weeks. I feel defeated, depressed, sad, and humiliated at the thought of being—well, I don't even want to go there.

I told Dr. Kaplan I felt like a fool for going through all the hell of chemo, thinking this was going to work. He said the chemo was still in the cards, because it was such a large tumor, and it most likely prevented it from spreading to other parts of my body. It is not in my blood or lymphatic system or anywhere else, thank God.

So, with removal of the breast, then, God willing, I'll be rid of the cancer. But it doesn't end there. I'm looking at a year of Herceptin every three weeks, which has to be administered like chemo, but there are no side effects. I was on Herceptin with my first round of chemo. It's basically to keep me from producing estrogen because of my HER2neu status. But that means I won't get rid of this damn port till the Herceptin is over. Plus, I'll be on sort of an anti-hormone therapy (which is a pill) to also suppress estrogen production (it feeds my cancer).

More aggravation: I will have to go through radiation. The risk of local recurrence is too great if I don't. That will start not too long after the mastectomy: every freaking day for, I think, six weeks. Am I having fun yet?

I can't start reconstructive surgery until after radiation, because the tissue changes—the elasticity and texture. I'm probably looking at two to three surgeries for reconstruction. Meantime, I guess I'll get a prosthesis, so that means when I go to Hawaii in December, I'll be sporting a fake boob under my swimsuit. I'm just sick about it.

I guess I should be happy that it's not spread, but all I feel is sore, of course, and sad.

To add to my horrible day, my ex mother-in-law, whom I have always loved, died today. Taylor told me as soon as he found out. She is the last of the four: —my folks and Ron's folks—and I am heartbroken. Taylor has no more grandparents. I am grieving this loss.

So, I'm in this for the long haul, I guess. Who will ever love me once I'm a mutilated freak? I am so glad I don't have to go through any more chemo, though. I had already decided I wasn't going to do it—regardless.

I was in horrible despair when I learned I would lose the breast. Joni and I cried and cried. She didn't want to leave me, but she had to go home after a week. Apparently, they knew in the beginning that the lobular cancer was a possibility.

After the lumpectomy. I was pretty sore and tired.

With chemo behind me, I was able to go to the dentist for a cleaning—it's too risky to do anything like that for fear of infection when you're going through chemo.

My eyes went really wonky on me too. I couldn't see that well at a distance again. So, I had to get new glasses. I decided to splurge on pretty new frames that exceeded what my insurance would pay, but at this point, I decided, what the hell. Later, my eyes would change again, and six months later, I had to get new lenses again. The new lenses were free, since I did it within six months. I had Lasix in 1999, but my eyes have regressed. However, they are still better than before I had Lasix. I was blind as a bat before.

Blog post: Monday, September 26, 2011
The Next Surgery

I have to make this quick—Dancing with the Stars is on in fifteen minutes! At least I can still enjoy my guilty pleasures!

So, it's set. My mastectomy will be on October 12. The first available date was October 11, and I just looked at Dr. Beatty and said, "Really—well, that's not happening!" October 11 is my birthday, and as if birthdays aren't bad enough anymore, I sure as hell didn't want to say goodbye to ol' leftie on my birthday.

This time, my sister Cheryle is coming from Alaska to take care of me. This will require an overnight stay in the hospital for me, and I will be very sore. Also, I'll have a drain for a few weeks—which totally grosses me out. So, she'll stay as long as I need her.

Dr. Beatty spent a great deal of time with me talking about next steps. My medical oncologist, the wonderful Dr. Kaplan, felt radiation would be a given. But then, my friend who had a double mastectomy called me and questioned why that would be necessary, since by removing the breast, they're removing the cancer—good question. She didn't have to go through radiation.

Dr. Beatty said they would radiate the chest in that area, but he also said the pathology after this one will tell the story.

As usual, I fall into a strange category. I had a huge tumor but had no lymph node issues. He said that's very unusual. The lobular cancer that is still there is a sneaky one. He used a cluster of grapes as an analogy. The grapes are the lobes that store milk, and the branches are the milk ducts. So, the cancer starts in the grapes and sneaks up the ducts; therefore, making it hard to see in imaging.

If pathology is super clean after this surgery, I can possibly skip radiation and move on to reconstruction.

If it's questionable, I suppose I'll have to do radiation, which will be a pain in the ass, because it's every day for six weeks. Also, they can't start reconstruction until six months after radiation, because it changes your skin texture. It has to totally heal. So, I still have a lot of decisions to make and much more to endure.

Meantime, there are prosthetics, and believe it or not, they recommend Nordstrom for the best prosthetic bras and fitters. Yay! I can put it on my Nordstrom card—and the insurance company will reimburse me. It's sort of bizarre—yes?

So, before my surgery, I'm going to be consulting with at least three plastic surgeons so I am armed with knowledge. Aah…Dancing is starting!

CHAPTER 13

THE MASTECTOMY

Blog post: Sunday, October 9, 2011
Tick-Tock

Three days until my surgery. I feel pretty good right now, but I will be freaking out more than likely Wednesday morning.

Picking up where I left off last time: It sort of sounds like I won't be able to get out of radiation. They just have to be sure that all the cancer is gone (since I had two different kinds of breast cancer). However, since radiation has to be every day for six weeks with no break, they won't start until I get back from Hawaii the middle of December. So, I will have plenty of time to heal from the mastectomy before they start radiation. Then, reconstruction can't start for at least six months after radiation—to allow time for the tissue to heal.

I've consulted with three plastic surgeons and have pretty much decided to go the route of a TRAM flap. I'm not interested in implants and having something foreign in my body. The TRAM flap is way more involved, however. They will move tissue from my abdominal area to form a new breast. It's a five-to-six-hour operation, with a three-to-six-week recovery, because you're cut in two places. But that's way off right now. I just have to get through Wednesday and the next few weeks of being very sore.

My psychological well-being changes from day to day. Thursday was horrible. I've been going along, hoping to God that my insurance company wouldn't "drop the other shoe," and sure as shit, they did—rat bastards.

Remember in the beginning that I opted to take part in a clinical trial? I did this to help womankind and do my part to end this horrible disease. Nowhere, absolutely nowhere in my insurance stuff does it say anything about clinical trials. Well, they are saying that somewhere in the fine print in the company's employee handbook, it says they won't cover treatment under a clinical trial. What that means is they are threatening not to cover the chemotherapy—which I couldn't even tell you what that adds up to.

Suffice it to say, I was devastated. I cried my eyes out and threw my cell phone, but now I'm just plain pissed. First off, I was never on any experimental drugs. Turned out, I was the control person, so I had the standard protocol. Second, any extra tests they did—MRIs and so on—were not even billed to the insurance company. I told them that. It doesn't seem to matter—the fine print is what it is. I totally do not have the strength to fight this alone, and I'm not. I've got people on it: the gal that represents Sound Publishing to the insurer, the social worker, my editor, and most importantly, Barry, the research nurse.

He called me late Friday and said he talked to the assholes at First Choice (my insurance company), and he said, "Man, are they mean." He and Dr. Kaplan have never heard of this happening—or even seen it. He knows how afraid I am of going broke over this, and he told me (and we'll wait and see) that they are going to squeeze whatever they can out of First Choice and then Swedish will pick up the rest. God, did that make my weekend more relaxing.

Still, I must say, insurance companies are all a bunch of crooks in my opinion. They sweet talk you, take your money, and then try to stick it to you. This country sucks when it comes to health care.

Nonetheless, I had a great weekend for a change. Friday night was the Washington Newpapers Association awards banquet—in Everett this year—so a bunch of us went. I had entered six stories, and I won second place in "News of the Weird" for a story I did about a human skull that was found at an estate sale. Figures: I'd win in the weird category! But it was a fun time. Then last night, my old pal Linell, whom I have known since the seventh grade, and a friend of hers, Pat, met me for a lovely dinner at Etta's. They bought me an early birthday dinner, so that was very sweet. Pat is a survivor and had some valuable advice for me. I was so grateful. Then, I met up with my pal Evan for a couple of drinks, and we got caught up, which was a lot of fun. And I had a good massage yesterday too.

So, this insurance thing is really bugging me. But they picked the wrong person to fuck with. I've worked my whole life. I'll be fifty-five on Tuesday. They are not going to ruin my life.

Evan: one of the first friends I made when I moved to Seattle. Such a little doll, but oh how he needs to grow up. He is still in my life—God knows why, considering the hurt I've endured at his expense. He has the effect of a bad drug on me.

Blog post: Sunday, October 16, 2011
What a Week

It seems like it was over a month ago since I last blogged, but it's been a mere week. And what a week it was. My sister Cheryle arrived Tuesday, which was my birthday. Seriously, it was one of the best birthdays ever. I worked four hours to get things wrapped up, and when I got home, I had two beautiful bouquets of flowers, tons of cards, messages on Facebook, and presents—it was almost overwhelming, and I thought, my God, do they all think I'm going to die tomorrow? I guess I really am blessed to have so many people in my life who really do care. Cheryle and I had an elegant dinner at El Gaucho, and she paid for my dinner, which I wasn't planning, but she insisted. So that was very nice.

Wednesday noon we were off to the hospital. I had not eaten, of course, and I had no liquids after 9:30 a.m.—so you get pretty grouchy by the time you get into the OR. We waited and waited. Finally, at 4:00 p.m., Dr. Beatty shows up—his surgery before me was complicated. I was supposed to be in the OR by 1:30. So, I just wanted to be knocked out and get the show on the road.

So, along with Dr. Beatty was this nice-looking young lady in scrubs. She was his resident, and I swear to God, she looked about maybe nineteen. I just sort of blurted out, "Are you old enough to be a doctor?" My God, we're talking Doogie Howser. She is a doll, and I learned later she is twenty-six. I said to her, "You must be very smart," and she said, "Either that—or very stupid!" So, I really dig her now too. The anesthesiologist came next: Dr. Higgins—cute little bugger. Once we got in the OR (I walked in and pretty much plopped myself up on the table—I'm skilled now), Dr. Higgins gave me the first little dose to make me relax, which is when I start talking about whatever is on my mind. I remember telling Dr. Higgins he was very cute and the nurses giggling that "the drugs were talking," then I asked if he was single.

The next thing I know, I'm in recovery, unable to open my eyes, but begging for ice chips. I guess Dr. Higgins decided it was time to shut me up. I never did find out if he was single! Sigh.

I got into my hospital room about 7:45 p.m. Cheryle told me that Dr. Beatty said my surgery was textbook: no complications. I still don't know what pathology will say. I will probably find out tomorrow when I go in for my post-op follow up.

The evening in the hospital was restless. I got so damn hot! So, I buzzed for the nurse and told her I was boiling hot—well, no wonder: the heat was up to eighty in my room! So, she turned it down, and I woke up freezing a few hours later. Plus, they came in at 1:00 a.m. to take my vitals and drain me. Hospitals really sorta suck, but they did have blueberry pancakes on the menu, which, oddly enough, I was craving, so I had blueberry pancakes and fruit for breakfast, which made me very happy.

The resident doc (the Doog) came in to check on me and the wound; that's when I pried her age out of her. Once they trained me on the drain, I was a free woman.

The drain is gross. It's a tube that goes directly into my chest, and this bloody fluid drains into a device that looks like a hand grenade—seriously. I've got it down now, but yesterday there was a leak somewhere, and we couldn't figure it out. So, we called Dr. Beatty's *answering service, and the Doog called back. She thought there might be a clot near the insertion point, and she said to take off part of the dressing to check it out. She was right. So, we stripped it from there all the way to the grenade, and I'm draining fine now. I have to write down how much fluid comes out. Once it's down to less than 30ml a day, the drain can come out. But we're looking at ten days or so. It's a pain in the ass, because there's a lump where it rests in a pocket inside my camisole, so dressing myself is a challenge. But once this sucker is out, I can get a real prosthetic bra and look pretty normal again.*

I'm feeling pretty well, though, but I sleep a lot. Last night, Cheryle and I did the Market Ghost Tour at Pike Place Market. There is a lot of paranormal activity there, and I had these two tickets and thought that would be fun during Halloween month. It was a blast. Our tour guide was a girl with the macabre makeup on and interesting attire. Her name was Kook! So we heard all the stories (many of which are truly fascinating) but never saw a ghost—bummer. After that, we had dinner at the Steelhead Diner at the market. We were home from our big date by nine, and I was tired. But I got out! We've watched a couple of good movies too.

Today, the big outing was Home Depot, Bakery Nouveau (a favorite little shop in West Seattle), and the grocery store for a few more items. I'm tired, but I'm so glad Cheryle is here so I'm not dealing with this on my own. She is going with me to see Dr. Beatty tomorrow. Tuesday, I think she'll head over to Shelton (on the other side of Puget Sound) to visit her brother and sister-in-law, and I'll attempt to go back to work.

On the insurance front, I need to call the attorney tomorrow to see where we're at. I did get a bill from Swedish for $138,351.00 in the mail Saturday and also twenty-eight pages of shit from my insurer. Cheryle crossed-checked all the dates to my appointment book, and indeed, they are trying to stick me with all of the chemo. They won't win.

I'm still going to Hawaii in December, but my son, Taylor—who turned twenty-one this week!—cannot go now because of an exam he has to take the day we were scheduled to leave. It's a state test for his EMT stuff, and he can't change it. It's too complicated to change everything now because of Christmas blackout dates and his school schedule, so I'm taking Colleen instead. We've traveled together many times and do just great together. But I will desperately need the break; then, I start radiation when I get back.

Meantime, I have to heal and get stronger. I had quite the whack to my body—literally!

I hated that drain so much. It hurt. And I still have a scar where its insertion point was. I feel like scar-body, like Al Pacino's *Scarface*. And I'll have yet another scar once I get the TRAM flap.

For my birthday, a package came in the mail from my friend Barrie. I was excited because it was from Nordstrom. Opening it with great anticipation, I pulled out a pretty, sexy negligee. I thought it was sort of in bad taste since I was having a mastectomy in a few days.

So, Cheryle and I went to Nordstrom, and I exchanged it for a really nice pair of pajamas.

When I was in my hospital room recovering from the mastectomy, Barrie called. I could hear Cheryle telling her we exchanged the nightie for pajamas, and I could hear Barrie from my bed saying something like "they sent what!!!"

She was pissed. Nordstrom, which rarely screws up, indeed sent me the wrong thing. They apologized profusely to Barrie after she got on them, telling them I'd just had a mastectomy and how could they send such an inappropriate item. So not only did they do the exchange, they went ahead and sent the pajamas she ordered, free, which were the same brand as what I exchanged the little sexy thing for, and they were both $80 PJs. I did well on that one now didn't I? Two fabulous pairs of pajamas that look more like loungewear, free!

I'll never forget Barrie's howling over the phone.

Blog post: Saturday, October 22, 2011
Tired and Sore

Everybody is asking, "How are you doing?" I'm tired, and I am sore. My big accomplishment today was to get Abbey to the groomer and pick her up. I didn't even shower until a little bit ago. I woke up too early, read the paper, had breakfast, paid bills, tried to make some sense out of hospital shit, and balanced my checkbook, and by then, it was noon, and I was exhausted.

I hate feeling so helpless and weak. My cousin, Julie, wrote in a card to me to "be patient with yourself." That is a very hard thing for me to do.

So, I'm already back in my jammies, eating an apple, and having a glass of wine, which I can tolerate again, thank God. But I limit myself to two glasses since I'm on pain killers.

What hurts so badly is where the nasty drain appears to start: sort of under my armpit, near the site where they took the sentinel node out, which hurt anyway. I hate this drain so much. They'll take it out when I get 30ml or less per day coming out of me. Today has been good: only sixty so far. It hurts, and it's ugly. My chest is ugly. All I'd have to do on Halloween is take my shirt off, and I could scare the living bejesus out of anyone. I hate the way I look.

The good news is that I am cancer free. I'm very, very relieved, but it doesn't make this pain any easier. I consulted with a second radiologist Thursday, and I will be doing radiation. It was a coin toss.

Since I was triple positive (for hormone receptors), there is a school of thought that radiation isn't necessary. However, with the size of my tumor and its aggression, it is recommended. I'm doing it. The day I made this decision, a story came out in the New York Times with the header: "Radiation Therapy after Breast Cancer Surgery Cuts Recurrence, Study Says." It blew my mind.

Basically, if I do this, there's a good chance it will never come back, and if it does, it will be in ten to fifteen years. By then, maybe there will be other methods of treating breast cancer. If not, well, I'll be old enough by then to just say screw it, go on a nice trip somewhere, and come home to die.

So, on November 9, I'll have a CT, which will enable the radiologist to know precisely where to aim the nuke, and I'll start radiation when I get back from my little trip to Hawaii in December.

I'm so proud of my kid. He rode all day the other day with the Coeur d'Alene Fire Department and took a few blood pressures and whatnot. I think he's really getting into this EMT thing, and I'm so happy about that.

I hope you all won't abandon me. Being cancer free doesn't mean the hell is over. I so appreciate everyone who reads this blog and cares about me.

CHAPTER 14

POST-MASTECTOMY

Blog post: Sunday, October 30, 2011
Another Week Goes By

I'm still hurting from the surgery, but I had a good weekend, and I'm feeling better about myself. The drain continues to be a horrible inconvenience, and the tubing is what really is hurting me.

I had to make a mad dash to Dr. Beatty's on Tuesday, because I was leaking so badly. My post-surgical camisole was pretty damp, and I freaked. It leaks right where it comes out of my body, so it's pretty awful. They redressed everything, and I'm using gauze and other dressings now, but they concluded I'm overdoing it, and that's why I'm leaking.

So, I've stayed off my elliptical and have just been walking. God, I hate this. I want to get back to Pilates so badly. But it has helped by my slowing down a little. I just want it out. If I haven't got to the point where it's less than 30ml a day coming out of me by the eighth of November, they'll take it out anyway, because it could start to be at risk for infection.

I also saw Dr. Kaplan this week—cried on his shoulder a little bit. He's just the best—they both are. We talked about my decision to go ahead with radiation and my continuing on with Herceptin, and he wants to get me on this anti-estrogen pill called Lapatinib (because of my positive hormone receptors), but it's a very expensive drug, so we're *going to be sure first that those assholes at my insurance company will pay for it. I won't die without it, but again, it will increase my odds against reoccurrence of the cancer.*

Swedish is still fighting for me on the insurance issue (they are trying to not pay for the chemo). I've put it in their hands. I cannot deal with it. It's too emotionally stressful.

Anyway, last week was busy: I worked more than I have in a while. We had the annual editorial conference Friday at the mother ship (the press facility and main office for Sound Publishing), which is almost to Everett. Actually, it was a pretty good conference—editorial staff from all over the place. I sat by the editor for the Vashon Island Beachcomber, *which got general excellence at the WNPA awards, and she is a wonderful woman. It's just her and one reporter—unreal. The keynote speaker was a Pulitzer Prize-winning journalist from the* Los Angeles Times, *who uncovered the city hall scandal in Bell, California, where the city council president and board members were bilking the city for hundreds of thousands of dollars for the salaries. Most city council members are paid a minimal "wage" for their services, and this guy was making almost eight hundred thousand dollars a day! I left after him; I didn't stay for any breakout sessions, because I was exhausted, so I left at 3:30 p.m. and got stuck in the worst traffic jam ever. It took me two hours to get home. I was so pissed! But the rest of the weekend was good.*

I have Herceptin Tuesday; then next week, a CT to figure out the positioning of the nukes for when they start radiation.

I'm getting more and more excited about going to Kauai in December! Barrie's coming too, so it will be two of my Alaska pals and me. It's going to be a wonderful reprieve for me.

The reason I was feeling better about myself, quite frankly, was that I actually had sex—yes, two weeks after the mastectomy. I didn't disrobe from the waist up—it's just too weird. No one would see this until I'm reconstructed. The person I had sex with was my old friend Evan, my occasional "friend with benefits." He totally understood and treated me with respect and tenderness. God, it felt good to be held. It had been a long time for me. I wasn't as energetic as I would have liked to have been, but for heaven's sake, I was still a mess. I get so lonely.

Blog post: Sunday, November 6, 2011
Where Has Time Gone?

How can it be November already? Today was a beautiful fall day: with lots of sunshine and beautiful colors, but it's cold! How could I have lived in Alaska thirty-eight years? But I did, and I still love it up there—in the summer!

I'm listening to the brand new Florence and the Machine CD, Ceremonials. God, I love her. Her voice is ethereal. This is the second CD from Florence. She is a fabulous English redhead. I was a redhead (my hair is coming back very dark). I am a quarter Welsh, so that must explain why I so love the royals and Florence! So, she is performing December 8 at the Wa-Mu Theater on a triple bill with singer/ songwriter Matt Kearney, then Seattle's own The Head and the Heart (who are fabulous), and then Florence is headlining. And guess who is in row thirteen, dead center in seat one? Me!—yay!

That's just two nights before I leave for my little Hawaii trip. Then I'll get back, and it will almost be Christmas. So, that's what I mean… where does time go?

Today was productive. That extra hour (going off Daylight Savings) is always such a godsend. The doctors, of course, keep telling me to take it easy, but it's hard for me—as everyone who really knows me, knows. But I was pretty good to myself this weekend.

Good news, though: I got that damn drain out of me Friday. I was still putting out more fluid than they wanted me to, but I basically demanded they take it out. It hurt. And it had been in three weeks and two days, and I'd had it with the fucker. I hate artificial crap in my body. I'm stuck with the port for at least another year, so that's bad enough.

One of Dr. Beatty's main nurses, Chris, took it out. It felt weird. She was very nice but also very stern and sort of a negative Nellie.

She wasn't happy with my decision to take it out early, because if my chest cavity started to fill up with goop, I'd have to come in and have Dr. Beatty drain it with a needle—maybe every two days, she said. Then, she said that if that doesn't work, they might even have to put in another drain. Meantime, Dr. Beatty is saying…well, none of that might happen.

Well, guess what? I haven't had to call him all weekend. I am not filling up with fluid. I win! I'm still sore and sort of feel like an elephant is sitting on the left side of my chest, but I'm healing well and, God willing, will be able to be fitted for a prosthetic in a week—yay again! I can even get a swimsuit with a fake booby for Hawaii!

The downer of the week was having Herceptin Tuesday. The Herceptin isn't the problem. For the first time ever, the oncology nurses were having a hell of time accessing my port. It was horrible. I basically got poked six times with needles: three Lidocane shots and three attempts to access the port. I was in tears. It seems my port has moved a little: it's crooked—probably from my chest area being jerked around in surgery. But, that was awful to say the least. (The port didn't move.)

Dr. Beatty is checking my wound again tomorrow, and then Wednesday, I have a CT to figure out where to aim the radiation.

I had a lovely late brunch today with one of my oldest friends, Linell. She's been so good to me. I've known her since the seventh grade. We went to this newer place in West Seattle called the Tuscan Tearoom, and OMG, it was fabulous! It's very girly-girl: with white linens, China tea pots and cups, fabric on the walls—you get the picture. We had a pot of incredible Amaretto tea, and then we both had Frangelico French Toast. I'm not kidding—died-and-gone-to-heaven good.

They do high tea and dinner too, and they also have wine. I'll be back! It was killer.

So back to time: I'm already worrying about Christmas. But, I bought three gifts today and already had a couple from a few weeks ago. So, yes, I feel productive.

Next weekend I will get a much needed baby fix, as my dear friend Erica comes to see me, with her adorable, precious almost-two-year-old baby girl, Quinn. I love that baby. I hope she'll warm to me and give me lots of love; I haven't seen her since April, so she may not have a clue who I am. I hope she remembers me. I'm proud to say I bought Quinn her first purse and her first faux-fur coat!

My own baby is doing fine. He's had to go through a lot of physical tests in order to even get into Firefighter I next semester, but he's doing well: healthy as a horse, my boy. Wish I were, too, but I'll get back to my old self one day. It's just going to take time.

CHAPTER 15

A VICTORY

Blog post: Wednesday, November 9, 2011
The Pressure is Off

This was a very good day. After having a three-dimensional CT to determine where the radiation "beams" will be directed at me, I had a wonderful meeting with the head social worker at Swedish about the insurance problem.

I can't believe this: I'm off the hook! She had already spoken to the director of corporate compliance and the director of the financial counseling department, and they said no way am I to be responsible for the $138,000-plus for chemo—that I'm not obligated to pay any of it!

We had to go through the formality of a letter and a financial questionnaire, plus a copy of last year's tax return, but I didn't have to disclose any value on my investments.

Based on my earnings from my job, I actually have made so little money—due to the reduced hours I've had because of all my time spent having all that fun in the cancer center and the hospital—I would be considered a hardship, and it's possible I won't have to pay anything else.

We'll see on that one. But this social worker, Sandy, is an absolute angel. She said she had been on vacation, got back, and heard about my case from Dr. Dobie (my shrink), and she was totally ready to take this on!

So, here's what will happen: Swedish will first go after First Choice, but if they won't pay (I assume after a legal battle), Swedish absorbs it. Swedish is sort of to blame, because they didn't check my insurance benefits to ascertain whether my chemo would be covered once I was in the study. But still, their attorney said federal law states they can't deny insurance for research study approved by the National Cancer Institute, which my study was.

At any rate, I'm off the study and off the hook for the big bucks, and I feel so much better.

It's one thing dealing with the disease and all the trouble that comes with it and another thing dealing with the possibility of never retiring—or worse yet, ending up living in my car.

More happy news: I was fitted for a form (or prosthetic) yesterday by a lovely, compassionate woman named Shannon at the downtown Nordstrom. My God, they whisk you into a huge dressing room and bring everything to you. She knew what the hell she was doing, as they are specially trained, and it looks pretty damn good. It's like a soft, gel-type thing, and it slides into a special little pocket in the bras. I got two really pretty bras. So, now I can wear my fitted clothes again and look like a girl!

I told Shannon about Hawaii, and they actually have a water form, so I am going to have them sew a pocket into my swimsuit top and get the water form—problem solved! She also said they can sew pockets into my sundresses that have shelf bras—another angel, that girl.

Oh, also—with Nordstrom, they bill insurance for the bras and stuff, because it is a prosthesis. No money came out of my pocket; however, the assholes (as I like to call First Choice) might deny the water form.

Also, I'm clear for Lapatinib, which they were hassling me about too.

I won!

My friend Erica came to visit with her adorable little girl, Quinn. Babies make me so happy, and this little one is special. They have their whole lives ahead of them.

Blog post: Sunday, November 20, 2011
Three Weeks until Hawaii!

I can't believe how time is flying! I have been tackling Christmas shopping with a vengeance, because I want it done before I leave on the trip. I can't believe Thursday is Thanksgiving already.

My sister Cheryle and her husband, Jerry, are coming down from Alaska for Thanksgiving. They are staying at Jerry's sister's house in Shelton, but we're all getting together at their daughter's home in Olympia for dinner. I'm picking up Jim, in Tacoma, on the way. It's been years since I've had a holiday with Cheryle, so I look forward to it.

I am getting stronger every day. Tomorrow, I have to go back in for a breathing exercise (called ABC) at Swedish to continue planning my radiation. Since it's my left side, of course they don't want my heart zapped, so this method involves a breathing technique that gets your heart farther away from the beams, and they tell me I'm a good candidate for it. I have Herceptin Tuesday, which is no biggie anymore—how far I've come tolerating all of this!

I was supposed to have a massage yesterday, but my massage therapist, Naomi, was sick, and I sure as hell don't want to catch anything. So next weekend, I have a pedicure, waxing, and a massage— all in preparation for Hawaii!

I also got the swim form for my swimsuit, and today, I'm picking up my bathing suit top and one sundress I have with a shelf bra in it that Nordstrom sewed pockets into for my forms. No one will know. I'm so grateful.

I also got a wide-brimmed hat with SPF 50 properties so I don't burn my head. I do have a pretty good crop of fuzz now—with no scalp showing—but I don't want to take a chance. Interestingly enough, my hair looks really dark! Lord only knows what it's going to look like in a year or so.

If you follow me on Facebook too, you will know that my dear friend Erica came to visit last weekend, along with her adorable daughter, Quinn, who will be two in March. Oh, we had such a good time, and that baby was so good for my heart. Erica was too. She gives good hugs, and I've needed that.

Have a wonderful Thanksgiving everyone. I am thankful to be cancer free this Thanksgiving. How about you?

Cancer free. What a weird concept after all I'd been through at this point: four surgeries (including the appendix mess), chemo, biopsies, tests, tests, and more tests. At this point, I was really looking forward to getting away—even if just for five days.

I did get approved for the Lapatinib, but I only took them for a week or so. I just couldn't tolerate them. One of the side effects is bad GI issues, but they also made me feel bad about myself: like I felt when I was going through chemo. I figured Dr. Kaplan would be pissed, but he said it was okay—not a life or death situation. Apparently, I'm not the only one who had quit taking them. I truly believe hormones have been the root of many of my problems my whole life. When I had periods, the psychological effects were horrible. I wouldn't plan anything that required social interaction, if possible, when I was expecting my period. I knew exactly when I'd start to feel wonky: withdrawn, depressed, anxious, impatient, and just plain sick.

How do men get off so easy?

CHAPTER 16

CANCER REALLY DOES KILL

Blog post: Saturday, December 3, 2011
Trying to Pace Myself

Thanksgiving came and went, and I've been going full tilt at Christmas stuff. But I had to slow it down a bit today, because I felt like I was coming down with a cold yesterday. I do feel better. I just got back from the movie, The Descendants, *and it is breathtaking. It's sad— and funny. It really got me excited though about Kauai, because part of it was filmed there, and I'll be there in a week! I can't even believe it. It's been so long since I've seen a warm, sunny beach.*

I need this break. It's been a rough couple of weeks. I start radiation December 19, which will be every damn day until February 1, and if that's not enough insurance with the Herceptin, well, I don't know. I just don't like the pills. When I don't feel good, I look in the mirror and hate what I see, and I just can't do that to myself anymore.

Tuesday, I received an email with news on Clarice in my support group. It wasn't good. She was in the hospital, and her husband didn't think she'd be coming home, as they had her on palliative care. She died Wednesday afternoon at four o'clock. I am still so upset by this.

She's fifteen years younger than I am and with two little kids. She had stage IV breast cancer, which had metastasized to her liver. They removed the part of her liver that had cancer, and she seemed to be doing okay the last time I saw her. I feel awful, because that was over a month ago. I hadn't been making it to group either because of work or because I was just too tired right after my surgery. But the last time I saw her, she gave me a hug. I am so confused. I don't understand how God could take a young woman with two children and a husband— and not me instead. These are things I don't understand. I will be at group Tuesday night, and I'm sure we'll all cry our eyes out. I have already cried over her and those kids. I mean, how do you tell a three-year-old that mommy's dead?

I soldier on. My Christmas shopping is done; I have my outdoor lights up and some decorations inside. I will put up a small tree when I return from Hawaii. I don't have it in me to put up the big mother. But Taylor is coming for Christmas, so I will put up a tree of some sort. He's still my baby, and I can't wait to see him. I will only have had one week of radiation by Christmas, so maybe I'll be able to ski with him.

I am getting stronger every day, and we plan to kayak the Wailua River one day in Kauai. I need some upper-body movement. I did start back at Pilates and am easing into it. We've also got a helicopter tour booked to fly over the whole island, specifically the Napali Coast and the Waimea Canyon. I don't have enough strength yet (or time) to hike to these mothers. But we'll do some shorter hikes.

So, if you're a Facebook friend too, I'll post photos from Kauai, since I finally stepped into the twenty-first century and got an iPhone. I'm getting the hang of it; I'm not exactly a tech queen!

And I promise to just relax and enjoy warmth, sun, and peace.

My support group friend's death was paralyzing to me. With her gone, I really didn't want to return to that group, because she was the only one I could really relate to, since we both had breast cancer, with similar experiences. She, too, had been on A/C and was the one who told me it was referred to as the red devil. She, too, had one breast removed. As it turned out, her doctors did a history-making robotic surgery on her liver, and it appeared to have worked, but they put her back on chemo, and she started to deteriorate. Her husband, who was so broken apart, wasn't sure if the chemo was just too much for her to take or if her liver just failed. He chose not to have an autopsy.

The rest of the people in the group didn't have children either. It was kind of weird. So, I don't think they got it when we talked about our kids—in my case, kid.

There was also one very annoying woman in the group, who actually depressed me. She had been cancer free (leukemia) for almost two years, but she was a downer. She constantly re-told the story of how she almost died, and even had a photo on her iPhone of her in the hospital in ICU with all these tubes and stuff. I thought that was sort of macabre. She whined a lot about how "I almost died," and we all were supposed to be sympathetic, then when someone else was talking, she would nod off. I couldn't take it anymore. Any one of us could have died.

I still go to Gilda's club. They have excellent lectures on everything from proper nutrition for cancer patients, to toxics in the environment, and other events.

There seems to be so much cancer in this world; it has to be something we were exposed to in the environment or some rotten preservative in food. I try to eat as organic and healthy as I can now.

But sometimes I wonder: what's the fucking point? To my life, that is. I love my son with all my heart. And I love Abbey, my first dog all on my own. Even though she can be aloof with me often (I don't know why she's like that—she can be a real snot), if it weren't for these two living beings, I really don't know why I'm here. I feel as though I should make space on this earth's growing population for someone smarter, healthier, and prettier than I am.

But I can't do it. It would be too selfish. There are those who love me and actually want me to stick around. But I'm so lonely. I want someone to love me; but see, right now, it's like: who the hell wants a chick with one boob? I disgust myself looking in the mirror.

CHAPTER 17

RADIATION BEGINS

*Blog post: **Sunday, December 18, 2011***
Radiation Starts Tomorrow

In Kauai with my friend and traveling pal, Colleen. We've been friends since the seventh grade.

I'm back from Kauai, and I hit the ground running. I had to get all caught up on mail and laundry and get a tree up, which I accomplished yesterday. It's darling: smaller than usual (because I just didn't want to fight with a big tree), but it's about four feet and is a very full and symmetrical Noble Spruce. I like it.

The trip was too short. Geez, for a small island, there's a lot to see! The helicopter tour the first day was money well spent. We got an overview of the entire island, which included the stunning Napali Coast, which you really can't see like that other than from a boat. We had such a good pilot. It was a little windy, but we never bounced around at all. We flew up Waimea Canyon (the Grand Canyon of the Pacific), up the Napali Coast, and very close to a volcano crater—everywhere. It was spectacular, and we never would have made it all by car or foot in five days.

I really scored on the condo. It was a Living Social deal; we were supposed to have a two-bedroom, two-bath, with a partial ocean view. Well, it was three bedrooms, three baths, corner unit with a wrap-around deck, top floor, with a full-on ocean view. They are really new and very luxuriously appointed: with nice furniture, granite counter tops everywhere, A/C, flat-screen TVs in each bedroom and the living room, full laundry, and housekeeping service. My bedroom (I took the master suite) had a bath of my dreams: huge tub, huge walk-in shower, two separate vanities, walk-in closet, and a safe. I loved it. It's called Koloa Landing at Poipu Beach, and it is a Wyndham Resort. They are for sale too, but holy crap, the two-bedrooms start at $925,000, and the condo dues—brace yourself—are $1,400 a month! Geez, that's more than I pay in rent! But I got this palace for $220 a night, and Col and I split it. At least I had five days living in the lap of luxury!

The other high point was my kayak/hike adventure. Because of my weak left side, I was worried when I started to paddle, but actually, it got better, and I am much stronger now and feel more mobility coming back. It was two-and-a-half miles each way, then a mile hike to "Secret Falls." The hike actually was the painful part! The trail was very slippery and muddy from the rains, so I had to tread very carefully. In addition, there were roots everywhere to navigate around. Once we got to the falls, they were spectacular. By the time we hiked back to the kayaks, it was clear that my right knee was hurting. It still hurts a little, but I went to Pilates yesterday morning and did some stuff that helped. But I didn't fall in the mud! However, my shoes and legs were covered in mud. For those who think I never get dirty, you would have been so proud! I was happy I challenged myself, and I made it.

So, we ate, drank, shopped, chilled by the pool, and went to the beach one day. The weather was sort of on and off, but it was fine. Just to be somewhere else was great—and to be with my dear friend Colleen. We had great fun the first night with Linell. She made the flight over a real treat too. She was working first class but would slip back to coach, bringing us champagne, then Mai Tais! We also got our food free. Thanks, Nellie!

Anyway, back to reality: radiation starts tomorrow. I'm sort of nervous, but I know it won't be as bad as chemo. It's just going to be a pain in the ass, because I have to go every day. After that, it will just be the Herceptin every three weeks until September 2012. And of course, reconstruction next summer sometime.

I still worry about the cancer coming back. I guess this is normal. The death of my friend in my support group has me thinking more about death too. I know I'll die one day, but I'm not ready yet.

In keeping with the spirit of moving forward and learning new things, I forgot to mention: I bought a ukulele in Kauai! I've been thinking about this for a while, and I thought, what better place to get one. I got it at a little place called Kamoa Ukuleles in old Koloa town. The owner designs all of them himself, but the demand has been so great, he's having them made in China now—unfortunately. His mom, Gigi, waited on me, and she was wonderful! They are shipping it, so I don't have it yet, but it's what they call a pineapple shape, made of mahogany. It's a starter uke (not terribly expensive), but I'm so excited! I think I can do this! I learned a few chords just standing there with Gigi. I'm having my nails done tomorrow after work, and they are going to have to be cut shorter for this to work. But it's okay. That is one of my goals for 2012: learn to play the uke, get well, and a few other gems.

Merry Christmas!

Little did I know that radiation would be so painful. By the end, I was peeling. Just getting set up for it was sort of a pain, but they wanted to see if I could do the breathing thing called ABC—where they zapped me on the inhale, so my heart was as far away as possible from the radiation. I did fine with the breathing. Apparently, some people can't do it; why, I don't understand.

Blog post: Saturday, December 31, 2011
Radiation Going Fine

I've had nine treatments now, and I am beginning to feel a bit fatigued—but not nearly as bad as it was with the second round of chemo. It's fast, and the technicians are wonderful. I go in the morning before work. I saw Dr. Kaplan this past week for the first time in about five weeks, and I told him I quit taking the Lapatinib, and he was okay with it. It's not life and death that I take it. It is an awful pill, and I just don't want to feel chemo-ish again. The radiation and Herceptin are good enough insurance that I don't get the cancer back. It was so good to see him. I was so used to seeing him every single week. He's still my main doc, and I feel safe (as well as hopeful) with him.

Christmas with Taylor was very nice: not too much drama, thank God. I love him so much. I worry about him every single day and probably always will. No matter how old they get, you can't stop being Mom. We had a lovely dinner out Christmas Eve, and then I cooked a free-range turkey on Christmas. I didn't gain any weight over the holidays or the trip, and I hope to lose ten pounds sooner than later—one of many goals for 2012, which I pray to the good Lord is a better year for me. I've had enough, right?

I had a very weird experience last night which still has me upset. Well, actually the weirdness started when I had a terrible nightmare Thursday night—well, actually Friday morning just before I woke up. I dreamed I'd been abducted and raped by these horrible people who were very dark beings. I was all cut up and bleeding. It was horrible. I shook it off and went to radiation and to work.

So after work, I went to a champagne tasting at the nice little wine shop, Bin 41, in West Seattle, which was fine. It was early, so I decided to get something to eat, since I've been eating turkey all week! I went to a very casual little place called West 5, because they make good fish tacos. It was still happy hour, so it was packed, but there was one space at the bar, so I took it. To my right was this guy that I gathered was named Scott, because the bartender knew him by name.

So, he said to me, "Why are you so cautious?" I didn't realize I was acting cautious, but this immediately put me on guard. He asked me what *my malady was. I looked at him and asked him what made him think I had a malady. He said he sensed it. So I told him I was a recent cancer survivor, still in treatment. It turns out he was a liver cancer survivor. Okay, good. But it got increasingly weird and uncomfortable. Apparently, he is a regular there, but they said he's not usually like that: dropping the f-bomb a lot and telling me that most human beings are expendable, that the world is in an awful place, and I wasn't voting for that fucking Obama, was I? The bartender told him to please not discuss politics or religion, which I appreciated. Then he started in on Roman Catholics, and I told him to stop, as I have good friends who are Catholic. He shut up while I ate, but I was so uncomfortable. Then he started back in, eventually telling me I would most likely die before him. At that point, the manager asked me if I was okay, and I said no. They finally ran him off and comped my drink. I was totally unnerved: waiting until I was sure he was long gone, beelining it for my car, and locking it as soon as I got in. They said he's "a little off"—you think?—and that he'd had too much to drink. Nonetheless, that's the first time I've ever felt threatened since I moved here. I came home and fell apart, especially when I drove up to the house and there were two raccoons staring at me. I just looked at them like: fuck off, and they ran. The whole thing was a nightmare. A fitting end to a scary year, I guess.*

I have no big plans for tonight—just a movie. I want to go skiing half day tomorrow. I haven't gone yet this year for lack of snow and time. I think I'm strong enough. I've been to Pilates six times now with my new teacher, and I feel stronger already.

Everyone be safe tonight and stay away from weirdos who tell you that you're going to die! That son of a bitch has no idea who I am.

Blog post: Saturday, January 7, 2012
Radiation Fatigue Setting In

I'm tired. In fact, when I get done here, I have to go lie down. My skin isn't burned, but the feeling of tightness is definitely exacerbated. Imagine how the skin of a drum is stretched over the frame. That's how my left side feels. I've had twelve sessions now, with eighteen to go.

I did go skiing on New Year's Day, and it was lovely. My goal was six runs, and I did it. It was a pretty mellow intermediate run, but it felt good to be out in the fresh air, listening to tunes through my iPhone and tuning out the world. I do feel stronger still, but this radiation is a drag on my energy.

When I get tired like this, I get weepy too. I don't want to be depressed; I've got too much to do this year to improve my life. I'm sort of overwhelmed with my list of goals, but I just need to take it one day at a time. I am determined to make this a year of healing, hope, and progress.

It doesn't help my fatigue levels either that as soon as the New Year began, work went nuts. Both my education beat on Mercer Island and city hall business in Sammamish are just crazy. I've got three night meetings next week. I told Mary, my editor, I will no doubt have to come home and rest in the afternoon if I'm going to cover all of this. Don't get me wrong—I want to. I love my job, and the school situation on the island is really a biggie: they're going to float a big-ass bond in April. I have so much fun with all of that. I know—It's kind of nerdy.

I have my first real ukulele lesson later this afternoon! I'm very excited. I'm having a hard time with positioning my hands, so I really do need help. I'm also having a pedicure for my "be-good-to-me" moment!

Happy New Year to all my faithful readers. You are all treasured.

CHAPTER 18

RADIATION IS NOT AS EASY AS I THOUGHT

Blog post: Friday, January 13, 2012
Fifteen Down; Eleven to Go

Radiation is getting old. Every freaking day is exhausting. I hit the wall earlier this week. I was so tired I was in tears. Suffice it to say I'm going to bed earlier whenever possible. Two nights this week I had meetings to cover, including last night (which was a doozy), so I'm toast today. Thank God, it's the weekend.

I saw my psychiatric oncologist for the first time in about a month yesterday. We had a good talk. It's amazing how she knows what I'm feeling. She reminded me that even though I am cancer free and done with chemo months ago, radiation is no easy task either, and that I am indeed still in treatment, so be kind to myself. She completely understood when I told her this past year (it's been almost a year since my diagnosis) seems surreal: it's like it happened to somebody else. I had cancer?

It's going to be a long time before I'm "back." She reminded me that it's okay to lower my expectations of myself—which I tend to place fairly high. If I can't complete all the goals I've set for this year, it's okay, she said. But I'm sure going to try.

My first ukulele lesson with my teacher was brilliant. He's very nice, young (thirty), cute (sigh), and patient! But I've been practicing the exercises he gave me and some of the chords, and I am totally comfortable with it and can't wait to learn more tomorrow. I've also been scouting out places this week. I want to move when my lease is up at the end of June. I want my own place. It will be ten years this April since I was officially divorced, and ten years since I was a homeowner. I'm sick of renting. I owned a home from the time I was twenty-one until ten years ago. I want my own place. I talked to a lender, and he thinks I can get a loan, since I've been on my job over a year now, in my given profession. The trouble is my limited hours in 2011 due to cancer treatment, but he said with proper documentation, I should be okay. The important thing is that I do have forty hours a week available to me; I just couldn't work them due to spending so much time at the cancer center getting treatments.

If I move by the end of June and get settled in, it would be perfect, because I'll probably have my reconstructive surgery shortly after that. That would be nice to recover in my own place.

I have scoped out a few places I will want to see, and I'm hopeful. I'm looking for a townhouse or condo, and I want to stay in West Seattle.

I also talked to my shrink about my support group. I think I need a different group. Ever since the one gal died, it's not the same for me. She also had breast cancer and had kids—I could relate to her. No one else in group has or had kids, and they all (for the most part) have some sort of blood cancer. And they're depressing me: too much talk of death, while I'm talking about moving forward. I almost feel silly trying to be positive. I've also talked to our group facilitator about it, and she said what my shrink says, and that is, if I'm not benefiting from it, then I shouldn't go. One gal in particular is just wearing on me. She's been cancer free now for over a year but is so damn depressing: constantly whining about everything from her job to the death of her partner five years ago to how she almost died. It's just too much.

There's a group starting up at Swedish in March for breast cancer survivors, and I think that will be better suited for me. Dr. Dobie said they take on issues about reconstruction, intimacy—all the stuff I'm worried about.

The memorial for our group friend that died is a week from tomorrow, and I'm sure most of the group will be there. I will tell the ones I want to know that I am choosing to move on to a group more suited for my needs.

Sunday, I'm going to the Broadway touring production of West Side Story *at the beautiful Paramount Theatre. I'm so excited! My co-worker Meghan saw it last night and loved it. Did you know it hasn't been on stage in thirty years? They've reworked it, and some of the songs are sung in Spanish now. And Meghan said the last number is way edgier than in the movie. I'm going with a friend, and I'm so excited!*

Anyway, I'm over half way now on the nuking!

The friend was Evan. He really enjoyed *West Side Story* and said he thought it was the best play he'd ever seen. We had a bite to eat after the show and, of course, sex. Naturally, I paid for most everything, because he never has any money—like I do (sarcasm intended). It was snowing like crazy that day, but being an old Alaskan with four-wheel-drive, I did fine. It was so romantic running through the snowy streets with him. I'll never understand my relationship with him.

Blog post: Tuesday, January 24, 2012
Sounding Like a Broken Record

In my last post, I said I'd hit the wall with radiation. No, now I have. I'm so miserable—not that anyone really gets it or cares. Maybe I am having a pity party, but I guess this blog is growing old on folks, because only a couple of people commented last time.

But as my shrink pointed out to me today (while I cried buckets of tears—which I've been doing now on and off for four days), radiation is still cancer treatment. Sure, I'm not losing my hair or toenails or puking, but my tissue is getting bomb blasted, and it's sore, red, and awful. And the fatigue has become worse. Pile on top of that the worst cold I've had in I don't know how long, and it's hard to be happy and normal.

I've had twenty-three treatments. Next Tuesday, I will know if that's the end or if I might have two more. At any rate, this will end next week. Then, I just have the Herceptin every three weeks, which is nothing in the relative scheme of things.

It will be one year, this Thursday, since I heard the words, "You have cancer." It's been a whirlwind. Did this really happen to me?

I came home today after the docs. I needed to rest. I've got to stop feeling guilty about missing work. Actually, I do a pretty damn good job. I spent four hours Sunday at a retreat of the Mercer Island School District's board of directors that was supposed to be last Thursday, but it was canceled because of all this crazy weather over here. I wrote a hell of a story, and my competition wasn't there. I don't totally suck.

The uke lessons are progressing. I get frustrated, because I can't move my fingers fast enough between chords, but again, I need to quit beating myself up, my shrink says. After all, I've only had three lessons. But it's the story of my life. I'm never good enough. I always "placed" outside the money, if you will. Sixth place doesn't win the trophy. It's a long story. I just want to be better at everything.

And then there was the memorial Saturday for Clarice, the sweet woman who died, who was in my support group. The sun came out and was shining brightly through the beautiful windows of her church—the Unitarian Church here in West Seattle. It was her. I was overcome with grief seeing her husband and little kids. There were so many people there who obviously loved her so much. I only knew her a short time, but I can't get over it. This shit does kill people. She was so smart—it's not fair. Her husband wrote a song about her before she got sick, and they played a recording of him singing and playing guitar to it. He's very good, and it just broke my heart. Then, at the end, a slide show of her life was set to the song "Say Hello to Heaven," by Temple of the Dog, and I couldn't help but smile—such a beautiful *rock song, so cool. I told my son to add that to my song list for my memorial someday.*

I hope it's not anytime soon, but we're all so vulnerable and really so alone.

CHAPTER 19

TRYING TO MOVE ON

Blog post: Friday, February 10, 2012
Moving Forward

I hope you like the new name (Survivor in Seattle)! I still have challenges ahead, but I did beat the monster cancer—at least for now. It's not unusual, I hear, to worry about the cancer coming back once you've been down this road. I even asked Dr. Kaplan Monday if he was sure I was cancer free. I am, but we are still taking precautionary steps.

Radiation turned out to be much worse than I expected. They really crank it up at the end, and as I write this, I'm peeling: like you do when you have a really bad sunburn. It hurts. But my physical therapist bid me adieu this morning, because my range of motion is almost back to normal on the left side. She just said to not force it and to be careful until my skin heals.

But I've been doing Pilates again at a studio that wasn't very convenient for me, but I liked the instructor. Well, guess what? An instructor I already knew, who is very good and is trained in authentic Pilates (as Joseph Pilates taught it) just opened a studio of her own— right above my office! Hello, convenience! I'm so excited, and she did a beautiful job on the space. So, I shall start with her Monday, and I have no excuse not to go. I consider that a blessing.

But, back to the healing: Understandably I am eager to get "rebuilt," but the plastic surgeon doesn't even want to see me until May 2. I wasn't really surprised. I need to heal before they start messing with me again.

Meantime, I have so many goals and projects to do, but it's all going to take time. I'm seriously looking at condos; in fact, I'm seeing a mortgage lender next week to get my ducks lined up.

I want to improve my life now. And the ten-year anniversary since my divorce and having to sell the dream home is coming up. Add to that the record-low interest rates and prices getting reasonable (even in Seattle), and I see no reason not to try.

But I've also been very frustrated this week. The ukulele I bought in Hawaii seems to be problematic. I bought a tuner and couldn't get it in tune. Scott, my teacher, noticed this before: the strings slip. I called the guy in Hawaii whose shop I bought it from, and he went on and on about how I just need to tighten the screws. Well, we did that to no avail. So, after work today, I took it to "Dusty Strings" in Fremont; they are the ukulele experts here. For thirty-seven dollars, including labor, they put new tuners on it, and it's fine! Yay! And…they have ukulele jams every third Sunday. I asked if I would be intimidated, and they said no; I should come! So, I will! I really like the little instrument. It's therapeutic for me.

I am also having fits with understanding my new computer. I bought a Mac Book Pro, and I love it—it's fast, fast, fast. It's just me. I have a class tomorrow at the Apple Store, thank God.

One day at a time. I have to keep telling myself that.

Blog post: Sunday, February 19, 2012
Making Progress

I always feel like there's never enough time for me to get all my stuff done on the weekends—or in life, period. I just do the best I can every day.

Today was a first. I went to the jam session for ukulele players at Dusty Strings. I was pretty nervous, as I didn't know what to expect, but I really did have a great time! There were many times I got flustered, because I still don't move quickly between chords, but I did my very best and had fun with it. Apparently, the leader today isn't the usual leader, but he's there a lot. He said he hadn't seen that many people there in a while. Then I heard someone say something about Eddie Vedder—funny. There were about a dozen women—from a quite elderly lady to very young—and two guys. It was good experience for me to play with other people and hear them; although, at times, I could feel the heat rising in my face, because I knew I was goofing up! No one seemed to care.

I didn't get to see a lender last week but have an appointment now on Tuesday to see if I can get a mortgage. I am so hopeful. I'm ready.

My old friend Jane and her husband, Ken, are in town for their daughter Jennifer's birthday, so I had dinner with them, Jennifer's boyfriend, and another friend of hers at Ray's Boathouse on Shilshole Marina, and it was so much fun! Then we went to a pub in Fremont (the Tin Hat, I think it was called), and more of Jennifer's friends showed up for her birthday. I had so much fun, and all the kids loved hanging with Jane, Ken, and me too. I was a little loopy and took Jane and Ken back to their hotel—big fun. I love it when old friends come to visit! And I love, love, love that Jennifer. She's such a sweetheart, and she and I are cut from the same cloth, as Jane says!

As far as my healing goes, I finally quit peeling from the damn radiation. The redness is getting better too. It's amazing. I had zero doctors' appointments last week and have none this week either. It's sort of freaky, because it becomes such a regular part of your life. Next week, however, I have Dr. Kaplan and Herceptin, then a follow-up with my radiology guy.

I did Pilates twice last week and did my elliptical for half-an-hour three times. I want my old self back!

So, I saw Evan a couple of times during this period, including the night after I was out with Jane and Ken, and had awesome sex. I didn't dare venture out beyond him—due to my one boob situation. At least he knows and accepts me. But he's a player and does, and did, break my heart. I couldn't help myself. I felt so stupid, because I was in love with him, but I knew there was zero future for a real relationship.

CHAPTER 20

GADS, GOULD I GET A BREAK?

Blog post: Tuesday, February 28, 2012
And Once Again, My Life Takes an Unexpected Turn

No matter what anyone says, your career, your job, is your identity. I loved this job, and I just got laid off today. I'm not crying anymore, but I feel pretty lousy.

Again, I didn't see it coming until I learned right after our staff meeting that Chad, our only professional photographer for four papers, was laid off. My next clue was that Janet, our publisher, was on her way to our office. She doesn't come over a lot. I was last in; so, first to go. I'll work until March 9—oddly, I started there on November 9, 2010. I don't want to go. Mary and I held each other and bawled later on. It's not her fault—or Janet's. It came from much higher. Each paper had to lay off one person. I don't know how Mary is going to do it, because I was the only reporter. She's the editor, but now, she's also the reporter. All that's left is sports, copy editor, and the ad "executive." Yeah right, like they're such executives.

It's just like when I got laid off at the Press. I have cultivated my sources both on Mercer Island and Sammamish to where I'm known, trusted, considered concerned, and accurate. Dammit, I hate leaving my beats. I'm so screwed.

I don't know what I'm going to do, but this is particularly devastating, because I had my arms wrapped around a sweet, sweet condo that I could afford. We were just waiting for my pre-approval, which is due any day now. I still want to know if they'd have given me a mortgage, but for now, my little condo has slipped through my hands, and I remain in this shit-hole. Not that it's really a shit-hole, but I just want a place with more light and in a better neighborhood.

Sweet Jesus, I don't know what I'm going to do. I guess I'll re-group, start looking for a job, and hey, I'll have time to work on my book.

For now, I could use a little love and encouragement if anyone's got it for me. These past ten years have been hell. Like Jack Nicholson said, "Is this as good as it gets?"

This, of course, is the book I was referring to. It may not be the longest book ever, or it may only appeal to other women who find themselves in this position, but I wrote it for myself too. I don't want to forget.

Blog post: Friday, March 9, 2012
Last Day

I'm pretty broken right now. Today was my last day at the Mercer Island Reporter. This was so extremely different from my layoff at the CdA Press (Mess). That one, well it was like: "don't let the door hit you in the ass." This time, my wonderful co-worker Becca gave me a card and gift that I couldn't open right then, she said. Well, when I did, it made me cry. Then, Mary, my favorite editor ever, stood at the door and waved as I drove off. We're all having lunch next week, along with the photographer who got laid off too. We're still loved, but the powers that be let us go.

However, I did apply for two good jobs today. Mary helped me dust off my old resume. Again, I cannot stress enough the difference in these two layoffs!

One of the jobs is with Boeing. That would be way cool, but their way of applying was screwy. It wouldn't let me upload my resume or a cover letter; rather, you filled out a bunch of screens. That's a bummer, because in my cover letter, I told them I have long followed their fortunes and, in fact, have 112 shares of their stock, which has doubled since I bought it. Plus, my papa was in the aviation business, and I've known the Boeing brand since I was a kid. But they'll never know. It's because looking for a job these days is awful. You can't meet a human being. I can't dazzle them with my personality! I really hate it.

Monday, I have an echocardiogram to see if my heart survived radiation okay. It should have, because I did the breathing method that kept my heart as far away as possible from the nuking. The ABC breathing method was interesting: you have a tube in your mouth (like if you are snorkeling), and when you breathe in deep, it registers on this machine, and then they zap you.

I am having acupuncture Tuesday—my insurance, which I have until the end of March, covers acupuncture, and it helped last week, so I'm going to go again. The mobility in my left arm is improving.

And while I still have insurance, I'm getting my teeth cleaned Wednesday. What else: Pilates, look for more jobs, spend more time with Abbey, clean house…. I'll keep myself busy.

Blog post: Saturday, March 17 2012
First Week of Unemployment

I had the echocardiogram Monday. The tech seemed to think my heart was working fine, but I'll know more Monday when Dr. Kaplan shares the results with me. I have Herceptin Monday, and then I'm seeing my shrink. It's good timing: I go from hopeful to hopeless one day to the next.

My biggest concern right now is insurance. It expires at the end of March, so I have two weeks to figure out what I'm going to do. When I was laid off from the CdA Mess, I went without insurance for a long time, but that's not an option in my current world of ongoing treatment and more surgery coming up.

I'm still waiting for the information on Cobra, so I left HR two phone messages and finally got an email that the information is "in the mail," but it looks like it's going to be $550–$600 a month. My unemployment is going to be $204 weekly. Yeah, right.

I have my investments, but I swear, if I ever end up totally broke, I'll check out.

I'm scared to go back on BHCCP, which is Medicaid, for fear of them going after my savings. The wonderful social worker I've been working with at Swedish says they can't go after assets unless I'm dead, but I've got an attorney and my financial guy looking into it.

Meantime, I'm having my will updated just in case I die in the next surgery or get hit by a Mac truck or whatever. And there are people out there who don't think we need radical health care reform—seriously?

I've applied for seven jobs so far: so basically, one a day since I've been unemployed, and I am hopeful with regard to one in particular, where I have a connection. At least I know more people this time. I'm no longer the "New Girl in Town," as this blog started out.

My ukulele playing continues to amuse me; in fact, I'm going to the Fremont monthly jam again tomorrow. I am also working on the book. In addition, I came up with a rather entrepreneurial idea last night that involves music, but that's all I want to say right now.

And I took some time out Thursday for some retail therapy at the newly relocated Nordstrom Rack downtown, and I got a few nice things relatively cheap! I bought a dress, thinking I'll get a job I can wear it to soon. It's pretty, and the neckline doesn't reveal all my battle scars.

This coming Thursday, I'm headed to Idaho to see my son and my old peeps over there. I am looking forward to this. I haven't been over there for a year. I was too weak to make the drive. I'll be staying at my friend Erica's; she has the cutest little two-year-old girl ever: Miss Quinn. Erica is having a little gathering for me—which I'm really looking forward to—with some of my old compadres from the Spokesman-

Review. Taylor and I are going skiing on the Sunday I'm there, and I'll see lots of other people.

I'm so happy for Taylor! He's doing really well in firefighter training and has a job interview the twenty-ninth of the month with the Idaho Department of Lands to fight wildfires this summer (which sort of scares the crap out of Momma), but it will be good experience and good pay.

I'm just going to a movie tonight. Maybe I'll stop and have one drink for St. Patrick's Day after the show. But tomorrow night is Evan's birthday party, and I have to watch my entertainment spending now— although, I already have tickets for two concerts and one Broadway play which were already bought and paid for before the layoff. I've got to have some sort of a life!

I went to the birthday party. It was in a private back area of a just-okay restaurant in Evan's neighborhood. I had never met any of his friends, so I was looking forward to meeting new people. Plus, I had gotten him a nice shirt for his birthday, because he always got his clothes second hand, and I thought it would be nice for him to have a brand new shirt; I got it at the Nordstrom Rack during my shopping extravaganza a few days earlier.

Evan's sister was there, and she was a doll—loved her. All of the friends gathered at that time were very nice. My first clue should have been when one of his buddies, a tall good-looking guy, said, "This ought to be an interesting evening," or something to that effect when he was introduced to me.

Evan is a different sort. He is unable to be monogamous for some reason. Fear, perhaps? Selfishness?—I don't know. Naturally, I am always safe when I'm with him.

He makes me laugh. He's smart and cute. Did I mention he's twenty years younger than I am too?

Everything was going fine, and then awhile later, a woman walked in. She was attractive but short and a little heavy: not bad. She was obviously older than Evan too. He likes older women. I observed their interaction carefully. I noticed her give him a book for his birthday. I could see him looking at it; then, he flashed me a look. I happened to be sitting where the few gifts that people brought were being stacked. So after awhile, I looked at the book. It was called "Cougar"-something and was clearly porn of younger men with older women. I slammed it shut and thought, oh my God, how tacky. I did end up visiting with her for a while, and she was actually pretty nice. But I knew she was one of his other lovers. She doesn't live in Seattle anymore but drove over from the Midwest (where she lives now) to check on a property she has here. She had just arrived in town that day.

After awhile, I got up to go to the restroom. To get there, I had to walk up a hall not visible from the party room. There they were: two inches apart. I came unglued inside.

I pretended I didn't notice, but I had to walk right by them. Jesus, it hurt.

I came back, got my coat, said polite good-byes to everyone, and Evan motioned for me.

In the same hall, he held me and kissed me, explaining he hadn't seen her in a while. He also said he loved me. I left.

When I got home, I texted him, "I love you. Happy Birthday." He responded around midnight with, "I love you 2, Linda."

This event—added to the job loss—began a terrible downward spiral into depression.

It would be a month before I talked to Evan in person. This is the typical pattern. I don't know why I put up with it. I think I deserve better. I did, on the advice of my therapist, send him an email to explain to him how hurt I was. He responded almost immediately with, "I have been super busy with work. I will call soon. I have been an authentic individual and communicated where I'm at. I care about you, Linda. Thank you for joining me at *my* birthday party:)"

I took the *my* birthday party to mean: it's my party, and I can hurt anyone I want.

I had been to a club with a girlfriend to listen to an awesome ukulele player and her band. I took my friend home and finally caught up with Evan; he actually had time to talk—at 11:30 p.m. I was so hurt, and he still didn't get it.

The reason I hadn't heard from him was because he was actually attempting a real relationship with another one of the gals at his birthday party. I was just stunned. I'm too old for games. Why didn't he tell me he now had a girlfriend? He didn't have a real good answer. I asked why he couldn't be in a real relationship with me, and he said that he and this other woman have a common vision/goal. I know what it is—and more power to them. But I don't think he's ever loved anyone like I have.

He tried to seduce me, but he acted torn about it. It seemed we were headed in the direction of sex, because he told me that he and his girlfriend had an open relationship, which I really don't understand. I know what that means, but I don't understand why anyone would want to have a relationship like that. What's the point?

But then he said something so shocking and off-color to me that I put my shoes on and had him walk me to my car. He made some crack about taking a photo of me naked and sending it to the new girlfriend. I was absolutely appalled.

I asked him if he'd really do that, and he said, well, no. But I wanted to go. I told him he needed to grow up. My heart felt like it had been ripped out of my chest and juggled and then put back in. I could hardly eat the next day and cried and cried.

All I could think was: please, Lord, tell me there is someone out there who will really love me, hold me, and understand my pain. Where is the compassion? People can really be hurtful.

Yet I was worried about him. I thought he might be in some sort of trouble; but I couldn't care anymore. It hurt too badly. He was just "somebody that I used to know," like the song says.

CHAPTER 21

ROAD TRIP TO SEE MY OLD "PEEPS"

Blog post: Thursday, March 29, 2012
Feeling a Bit Renewed

The trip to my old stomping grounds was good for my head. It was not without some drama: going over—although the weather was picture perfect—there was a snow slide just past Snoqualmie Pass, which delayed traffic for two hours. So I had to hustle to get to Rathdrum, Idaho, to meet with my financial advisor about Cobra and how to survive, and he waited for me—bless his heart. I didn't get there until 6:00 p.m., but we had a good meeting. I decided it would be wiser for me to pay the Cobra than go on any kind of state assistance and risk the government coming after my assets.

I got to Erica's at eight o'clock, totally exhausted, only to realize I left my green bag at home—with all my meds in it. I freaked. I could not believe I was that spacey. I called my pharmacy (QFC), which is a Kroger store like Fred Meyer, so I was able to get some pills I absolutely needed at the Coeur d'Alene Fred's, but it cost me forty-seven dollars. Meantime, darling Alex, who works in the office here at West Ridge Park, went into my apartment with my blessing, and sure as hell, the bag was on the floor in the bathroom. He shipped it off to me UPS, and it was to arrive the next day before noon. Well, some dipshit Saturday part-timer said there was no such address, so I didn't get it until Monday, the day before I came home. Poor Alex, he paid to send it to me out of his own pocket: eighty-eight dollars. So, I went to the office yesterday to pay him back, and he said, "Oh let's just wait," because he already had started a battle with UPS, so hopefully, they will refund the whole thing. Erica does live at a rural address, but she's not off the grid, for heaven's sake!

After the first night's fiasco, however, it turned out to be a lovely time. I got to snuggle with Quinn a lot; she's Erica and Matt's adorable two-year-old cutie pie. She's so sweet, and she was fascinated with Abbey and me. She loved all my sparkly jewelry. Babies are so special.

And my baby, all of twenty-one now, is doing well. We had a lovely lunch the first day with Kody (his best friend from middle and high school, who is like a second son to me) and gossiped about their old high school gang. It was so much fun. That evening, Taryn, Erica, and I had a girls' night at the Oval Office, a yummy restaurant in Post Falls, and talked for hours. They gave me a little tough love, but I needed it. I love them both with all my heart. Working with them and the old gang at the Spokesman Review was one of the best job times of my life.

Then, the big party was Saturday night at Erica's. Neither of us slept well Friday night: Quinn had nightmares or something, and Abbey was driving me nuts, snorting at me half the night. But we managed to pull it together and had a nice spread for folks to make panini. I was so tickled—all the old Spokesman crew I worked with came, and so did one former colleague from the CdA Mess, who is now at the Spokesman. Jesse even brought his ukulele (he's very good), and we played some songs together, and it was so nice. He was patient and encouraging for me, and everyone seemed to enjoy our efforts. (Thanks Jesse, I really appreciate it!) The party started at 4:00 p.m. and wound down about 11:00 p.m. And little Quinn, in her cute pink skirt and matching cowboy boots, partied like a rock star the whole time. She doesn't want to miss a lick!

Sunday, Taylor and I skied half day at beautiful Schweitzer Mountain, just north of Sandpoint, Idaho. Oh my God, it was so gorgeous and hot! I had borrowed some long underwear from him—big mistake. I was roasting to death. Fabulous! Great snow, good time—except he always kills me on the first run. He forgets I'm thirty-four years older than he is, and I'm still recovering from cancer torture. But we got in four good runs, and my legs were getting rubbery, so I figured it was best to quit before I hurt myself.

After skiing, we stopped in Sandpoint; I forgot how totally groovy that town is. Taylor wanted to show me a rock store he loved, and holy crap, it was fantastic! Every imaginable rock you can think of, including a huge natural crystal brought from Brazil with rose quartz in the center. Seriously, you can't even get your arms around it.

Monday was divided into visiting three different friends: first, lunch with an old high school pal, Claire, who moved to Coeur d'Alene after I left. So that was wonderful. Then, coffee with my friend Penny and more coffee with another old pal from the CdA Mess (who no longer works there) who also has a new baby I got to hold. It's like babies energize me. They have their whole lives ahead of them. I just hope it's a better world for them.

Meantime, of all the ironic things that can happen, I have a job interview tomorrow with…my old employer, Sound Publishing; yep, the same ones who laid me off. A gal quit, but I have to go through the formalities again. The bummer is that I'd be in the Bellevue office, and I really don't like Bellevue. It's too stiff. Seattle is hip, where Bellevue seems plastic. But I'd be the assistant editor of their A&E mag, which is right up my alley, among other things. So, we'll see.

Meantime, Taylor had his big interview with the Department of Lands in Idaho today—to fight wildfires this summer—and he said it went well. God, I hope he gets it.

I went to Gilda's Club tonight for a lecture about our toxic environment and how it could be affecting our health and lives. It was pretty good. Stay the hell away from all pesticides and tobacco and watch labels. If a product has the words danger, or poison, do not buy it! Also, get this: PVC, like in many home pipes, is a killer too. It was funny, because the speaker had a bag of props, and he pulled out one of those long plastic guitar-shaped vessels they serve crappy margaritas in at the Gorge and said they are entirely made from PVC. As soon as he took it out of his bag, I was like, oh my God, the Gorge margarita vessels! Everyone laughed, because I immediately recognized it. I told *them the margaritas taste like shit too! So, there it is. The margarita in the PVC guitar-shaped container is why I got cancer!*

So, I'm getting a good deal of exercise, have dropped a few pounds, and feel pretty good—just tired right now. I'm excited, because my friend Christina and I are going to a special concert by the Seattle Men's Choir Saturday night. It's called "Come Together," where, for the first time, they will perform all Beatles songs—can't wait; they are so fantastic. We're having dinner first at The Melting Pot, which is always fun—it's a fondue place.

I've applied for eleven jobs total now, not including tomorrow's interview with my old employer. I will continue to hold out hope for an improved life. There's only one doctor's appointment next week—yay!

CHAPTER 22

BAD DRUGS

Blog post: Wednesday, April 11, 2012
Unemployment Sucks; Anxiety Almost Paralyzing

It's been almost two weeks since I blogged, and I still don't have a job. The interview with my old company—for the Bellevue position—went great, but they still haven't hired anyone. Go figure. I had a phone screen with one other company which was basically a few general questions from a recruiter, but she said they'd filled the position but would keep me on file for an interview should another opening come up—weird.

It's so frustrating—not to mention, scary. So meantime, the shrink decided to put me on Wellbutrin in addition to my anti-depressant I've been taking for years—which was a huge miscalculation on her part. I threw them out almost a week ago after I found myself seriously thinking about how to end my life. I went to a pretty dark place: looking on Google, for example, on painless ways to do it. I'm quite sure the pills were part of the reason. I could never understand the warnings about some anti-depressants making people suicidal, but now I get it. I guess she thought it would help, because I've been pretty low about the job situation, as well as a family matter that shook me to the core a week ago.

I'm now in a new group called ABC, or life After Breast Cancer. I'm finding it to be much more helpful than my old group. We talked a great deal last week about what we need to get better. I need peace and not to have to deal with other people's shit right now. Our facilitator, Jacci, said that's perfectly fine. Even though I'm "cancer free,"—whatever that means—I'm not over all of this. I suppose it has changed me forever. I found myself drinking too much (alone at home) after the layoff, so now I don't even keep it in the house. I had two Mimosas while sitting in the sun on Easter, and that's it this week. I also went to a different church than the one I have gone to previously here (not that I go very often), and I felt a real connection to the pastor. He was greeting everyone as we left, and I handed him a prayer card for his eyes only.

He emailed me, and we've been having an email conversation. I haven't ever done anything like this. But I need faith right now, and it's slipping away. He's going out of town for a couple of weeks, but when he gets back, we're going to visit in person. I just have a good feeling about him. He's not some sleazy preacher. It's a Lutheran church, which is fine. I was baptized in the Presbyterian Church, but I've always considered myself a "jack Presby!" Taylor was baptized in the Lutheran Church, where my dear deceased mother-in-law went to church.

This week, I've had doctors up the ying-yang. Monday, I had my three-month follow-up with my breast surgeon, Dr. Beatty. He said I'm healing well. I asked about the occasional shooting pain in my chest cavity, and he said it's normal: nerves are reconnecting. I'm still basically numb throughout the left chest area, but my arm is getting back to normal.

I don't see the plastic surgeon about reconstruction until May 2, but Dr. Beatty thought, from what he saw, that I should be able to have reconstruction in July, which is kind of what I thought. I cannot wait. I know it will be another long healing process, but I hate the way I am now. I'm working out regularly, eating well, and starting to get real strength back so that I can go into reconstruction healthy.

Also Monday, I saw Dr. Kaplan and had Herceptin—no big deal anymore. Then yesterday, I saw an ob-gyn for the first time in two years for the dreaded check of my other girl parts. Dr. Kaplan referred me to this gal, Dr. Pray. I loved her—young, awesome chick. I'm sure I'm fine. My maternal grandmother died of cervical cancer (I never knew her), but Dr. Pray said cervical cancer is not hereditary. Whew!

I have my group in a little bit, then Friday I see the shrink again, and I have a mammogram on the remaining boob. I couldn't believe imaging when they told Beatty's nurse I'd better have both sides done. I looked at her and told her to tell them there's nothing to "mamm" on that side—idiots. They obviously hadn't read through all my health records. It's all there in Swedish's system.

I continue to attempt to play my ukulele; I even went to another jam Sunday afternoon with the Seattle Ukulele Players Association. It was fun, but I still struggle to keep up, and this group does a lot of Hawaiian stuff, which I don't know at all. It helps to at least have the song sort of in your head.

It was also very wonderful to spend last Thursday with an Alaska pal, Marilyn, who was in town for the day on a long layover. We sold real estate together back in the day. We went to the Gauguin exhibit at the Seattle Art Museum that's only here until the end of the month. It was "first Thursday," so it was cheaper. It was a very good exhibit: works from his time in Polynesia, where both Marilyn and I have been. She's a lovely person.

I think I'll go to one of the Mariners' opening home games this weekend. It's supposed to be another nice weekend—last weekend was beautiful. It's supposed to be the warmest on Sunday, so I think I'll see about getting a ticket for that game. I love watching them live. And the cheap cable I have doesn't include ROOT sports, which is the channel that carries their games. I think that sucks that I live here and can't even watch them on TV. It's like when the Olympics were in Vancouver—what, three hours north at the most—and we couldn't watch any of the events live. I don't get these things.

If I don't get a job pretty soon, I'm thinking of running away for a few days to the San Juans—for peace.

I booked my old glampsite at Lakedale Resort for Memorial Day Weekend. I knew it would be busy that weekend, but if I did get a new job, that would be my only opportunity to get away. Lakedale Resort is on San Juan Island; this would be my third time there. As far as searching for my faith, I didn't ever go back to see the kindly pastor. It's not that I don't have faith, and I do believe in God, and I do pray on occasion. I just felt weird talking to clergy, because I've never read the entire Bible, and I don't want to feel stupid.

The Bible, in my opinion, is a tough read. Certainly parts of it are lovely, but I just get slogged down in it. I know God loves me; I'm just not sure how to communicate with Him or Her effectively. I've been a good person, and I try to do the right and honest thing. I believe that those qualities—and love—are the basis of Christ's message.

Blog post: Thursday, April 19, 2012
Out of the Abyss

Things just kept getting worse with my mental state after my last post. I saw Dr. Dobie the day after my last post, and she mentioned she had also noticed a change in me since Dr. Kaplan put me on the estrogen blocker. Then, I had a grim reality to face Friday night, which I won't go into here. Suffice it to say I realized someone I really cared for, really doesn't give a damn about me.

By Saturday, I was back in the rabbit hole: thinking about death. The sun was out, so by four-ish, I ventured out of the hole to the park with Abbey and talked to the trees, God, and Joni by phone. I felt better, but I still wasn't finding my joy.

Sunday, I went to the Mariner's game. I had a great seat, it was good weather, and they won. But I came home and cried. By Monday, I called Dr. Kaplan and told him I thought the estrogen blocker was making me crazy. He said stop taking them and come see him in a couple of days, which I did. I've been off them now three days, and I feel so much better. I'm finding humor in weird shit again (that's the real me) and enjoying my ukulele—even singing while playing (don't ever ask me to sing in front of you)—and marveling that I'm remembering several chords and don't have to look at my hands. I'm back.

The mammogram on my right breast came out A-OK: nothing to worry about there. My other girl parts are fine too: no sign of cervical cancer. I'm doing my Pilates, and I am back up to forty-five minutes on the elliptical at level seven. I've even lost a few pounds and moved my belt in one notch. The new support group is so good. Last night, we got onto the subject of intimacy after cancer. It was hilarious. I felt like I was back in my fifth grade (or whenever it was) sex education class. Jacci uses those gigantic Post-it® notes to write stuff and then sticks them on the wall, and one had these words: vibrator, masturbation, and something else in a row, and I said, "God help the janitor; he's going to wonder what the hell went on in this conference room!" It was so open and cleansing though. It's a tough issue with body image problems.

Anyway, before the Friday night incident that I won't go into, I went to The Pink Door with Sophia (my little young friend who goes to UW) to listen to Miss Rose and the Rhythm Percolators. Miss Rose is an awesome ukulele player, and I loved her! I was in awe watching her hands, and she sings beautifully too. Her uke is solid ash: a canoe paddle shape. I introduced myself and told her I have a repertoire of four songs—period—and she said that was good! She leads the jams at "Dusty Strings," but the only time I went to that one, she had a substitute. I'll go to hers next month.

I actually got the courage up to try the online dating thing again, too—not Match; Lord, no. My friend Lisa told me about a free one called "OkayCupid," so I've already been chatting with a couple of guys. I might have coffee with one this weekend. He seems nice. Another one (a real hottie) obviously just wants to have sex, and I'm just too vulnerable for a casual hookup right now. My heart gets broken too easily. Men: don't even get me started.

I didn't get the job in Bellevue. I keep looking. I'm not losing hope yet, and now that I'm off those awful drugs, I feel in control of my life again. I see Dr. Kaplan again on the thirtieth for Herceptin, and we'll re-visit the hormone thing again. He believes I need to be on some sort of estrogen blocker because of my positive ER/PR markers, but obviously, that one wasn't the right one. I told him that when I did have menses, I suffered from horrid PMS (depression, couldn't think), and that's how I felt, so we've got to avoid that again. If nothing works, I just will go without the hormone treatment altogether. It's not an automatic death sentence, and I'd rather live with a clear head then think about how to off myself.

The Friday night incident, of course, was about Evan. He had finally made time to grace me with his presence. Of course, it was late, and I didn't mention before that he scared me. When I got to his building, a sort of shady-looking black dude was outside the door, and Evan really ripped into him, telling him to get the fuck off his block, etc. I asked him "What the hell was that all about?"

Oh, he was a crack dealer and he didn't want him there. But I'd never seen him like that. This was the conversation where he told me he was attempting a relationship. Anyway, this one dude online that was just interested in a monthly hook-up reminded me so much of Evan: not in his looks, but just that sport-fuck mentality. They can go to hell.

CHAPTER 23

THE DRUG PROBLEM GETTING BETTER

Blog post: Tuesday, May 1, 2012
Feeling So Much Better

Mentally and physically, I'm much better. I saw Dr. Kaplan yesterday for Herceptin, and he's giving me another three-week reprieve before we try another estrogen blocker. This one will be in a different family of drugs, so hopefully I won't spin out. I couldn't take it again.

I always tear up when I have life and death conversations with him, which I usually initiate, but I have to know my odds. If I can tolerate another estrogen blocker, I increase my chances of the cancer not coming back by five percent. To me, that doesn't sound like a lot. But I'll give it a try in three weeks, but if nothing works without me feeling so dark again, I won't do it. I said to him, "You know that bumper sticker that says, 'I'm low on estrogen, and I've got a gun?'" Well, that's how I felt. Only I wouldn't shoot somebody else. I'd shoot myself, and I don't really want to do that—too messy! I know: sick.

I am very excited about tomorrow for many reasons. First, I finally get to see the plastic surgeon again about reconstructive surgery. I'm so anxious to hear what he has to say about when we can do it. I so desperately want to be "normal" again. I've waited months for this appointment.

Also, tomorrow, my friend Barrie (whom I have known forever) and her daughter, Jenny (whom I've known since she was a toddler) are flying in. Jenny is expecting her first child, so they are coming down from Anchorage to shop for baby furniture and all things baby. I haven't seen Barrie since Jenny's wedding in the summer of 2010. Jenny was down last fall before she was pregnant. So, it will be so much fun to see them both. Barrie's staying here Thursday through Sunday; Jenny's staying at her friend's home in Olympia, but we'll all get together.

Meantime, there's still no luck with the job hunt. I received yet another rejection email today. It's beginning to feel like 2009 again. I had some other ideas, and Jacci, our group leader of the After Breast Cancer support group, encouraged me to think outside the box. So, I sent some emails regarding this idea, and not one has responded. It's terribly discouraging, but I am just trying to keep the faith.

Meantime, if you're a Facebook friend, you probably saw my photos from this past Sunday's Beams and Dreams sailing adventure. It was so much fun! I was alerted to it by Gilda's Club and got in and was able to bring a guest, so I brought my crazy pal Mira. We crack ourselves up—we both think we're so funny! Anyway, Beams and Dreams was the brainchild ten years ago of two brothers, then twelve and thirteen, as a way to give back. It's a free sailing adventure for cancer patients. Their parents were on the trip as ambassadors for their sons, who are now in college. These boys, at such a young age, sent out hundreds of inquiries to make this a reality, and hooked up with the Adventuress, a monster of a sailboat, built in 1913 as a whaling ship.

Now, the Adventuress is a nonprofit, mostly used for teaching and research. But we got to help out raising the sails and whatnot; I can't remember all the terms, but Mira and I decided it was all about jibbing and jabbing—of course, cracking ourselves up. The crew was so nice. The captain was way cool—I told him he needed a parrot on his shoulder! Anyway, it wasn't real windy, but we eventually caught a breeze, so they turned the engine off, and we bobbed around Elliott Bay. It was lovely. Very good for my soul.

Next Tuesday night, Mira and I are going to the Black Keys concert at the Key Arena. Rock-n-roll! I'm so excited! They are so freaking good! I'm sure we'll have a blast. I've got my personal summer concert *lineup mapped out: in June, I'm seeing the Broadway production of American Idiot at the Paramount—yes, it's a play, but it's scored by the rock band Green Day. I scheduled nothing for July, because that is when I suspect I'll have my surgery; but then in August, I am seeing Melissa Ethridge as part of the Zoo concert series then Aerosmith at the Tacoma Dome! I haven't seen either of them since the nineties—at the Spokane Arena. Melissa is a breast cancer survivor and one rockin' chick. Then, in September, I'm super excited about seeing Bonnie Raitt at Chateau Ste. Michelle winery. I have loved her to death since the seventies, and I haven't seen her since the seventies in Anchorage! Her new CD is stunning.*

So, the music keeps me going.

The online dating is pretty weird. I did have coffee with this one dude, and he talked about himself for the entire hour—then had to split. I could tell he wasn't interested, but I wasn't either. Good God, he's sixty and still has fucking roommates. Grow up, dude. Then, there are the ones who get to chatting with you online, and then you finally realize they are only interested in a FWB—ever heard that one? I hadn't until a year ago; it means: friend with benefits. No thanks. Again, grow up.

My hair continues to amaze me. It's dark and curly! It was pretty much stick straight and blonde as a child; then it got more brownish-red, so I enhanced the red for years. Now, it's dark, dark brown with amazingly little grey. I had to have it trimmed and shaped last Saturday, because I was beginning to look like Little Richard back in his pompadour days or an eraser head.

I'll update soon regarding the next surgery. Peace out.

CHAPTER 24

RECONSTRUCTION SCHEDULED

Blog post: Thursday, May 10, 2012
Surgery Scheduled

Well, this whole reconstruction thing is going to be another long ordeal. I go in a week before surgery for what they call "delay." This is to mess around with blood vessels in my abdominal area to increase the blood flow to the area so it's nice and supple. I will be knocked out and will be sort of woozy for twenty-four hours. This procedure is because Dr. Isik will be using belly fat and muscle to construct my new left breast. It's really pretty clever—I get a tummy tuck too! Then on July 23, I have the TRAM flap. It's about a six-hour surgery, and I'll be in the hospital one or two nights—no kidding. I'll be toast for a good two weeks, and I can do no strenuous exercise for eight weeks—which is going to suck. So, I'm really trying to get into fighting shape before this happens. I will have friends coming in shifts to care for me. This will be my hardest surgery yet. But I don't want an implant. I don't like the idea of a foreign thing in my body. Besides, most women reject them in ten to fifteen years. This way, it's made from my own tissue, so my body will not reject it.

There are three more in-office procedures after that: all about three months apart. They involve symmetry and the creation of and tattooing of a nipple. I was pretty emotional, because I didn't realize that I'm still in this for the long haul. So, one more year of my life will be sucked up by cancer crap.

Meantime, Barrie was here from Alaska, and we had a marvelous time! We had a wonderful lunch over the water at Defiance Point in Tacoma for Jimmy's birthday, along with Jenny and her friend Maria, who lives in Olympia. Barrie came back to Seattle with me, and we shopped, ate, drank wine, and just had a great time together. I still get tired from too much, and I was a little pooped when she left Monday.

I had barely caught my breath, then it was Tuesday evening, and that meant the Black Keys concert at the Key Arena. My God, they are so incredible! The sound quality in the Key can be a bit iffy, and this time it worked for some reason. It was a fabulous show: with the guys performing most of the songs off the two most recent CDs, Brothers and El Camino. I was with Mira and her friend Juan, and I was on a first date with a very nice man named Dave. We all had dinner before the show. Dave said he had a really good time and enjoyed the company. It looks like we're having dinner again Friday night. But I'm moving slowly. I've suffered too many broken hearts in my life, and obviously, I'm in a different head space now since the cancer. I've got to protect myself and do what makes me happy. I'm very independent—geez, as of last month, I've been on my own now for ten years. I just don't want anyone to try too hard. It has to be natural. I am who I am. I don't expect anyone to change for me, but they damn well better understand me.

We finished up my ABC support group last night, and if I learned anything from that class—and I did—it is that everything I've felt is completely normal. Now I have to figure out how to move forward in my new normal. This includes taking care of me physically and mentally. I cannot and will not tolerate any outside bullshit.

At the Black Keys concert, in my new "hippie chic" ensemble.
I was happy and having a good time. And I felt pretty for the first time in a very long time.

Remember me mentioning Miss Rose and her band at the Pink Door a month ago? Well, I took a ukulele lesson from her yesterday! It was awesome! She's so cool and sings so beautifully, too. I told her not to expect me to sing! Actually, when Barrie was here, I drug her to my favorite dive/karaoke bar, and I did do one number—yes, Taryn—my infamous "You're So Vain!" Barrie about died! Some old cowboy coot grabbed her and made her dance with him while he sang a country tune. He was very good, and it was hilarious watching Barrie! Anyway, my old uke teacher, Scott, really did get me far, but he's really a guitar teacher, and there is a big difference. Miss Rose (Sunga) is having me learn some scales, and she also thinks I should cut my nails down. I'm sure she's right, but I'm not going to do it myself and flip Christina out (my friend and nail tech). I'll let her do it! But it will make it easier on

certain chords where three or four fingers have to be on the same fret.
So, I'm taking another lesson from Sunga next week, and then her jam
session is on the twentieth at Dusty Strings. I'm psyched!

I'd be more psyched if I could find a job, but geez, this week some
really, really interesting ones have popped up that I believe I would be
excellent at. One is with Zillow, a real estate website, looking for an
editorial writer. It's a contract gig but could work into more. I mean...
hello? I was a real estate professional for twenty years and have been
a journalist for ten years! I told them in my cover letter, "I'm your girl!"
Don't you think?

Dave forgot about asking me to dinner Friday night, and he didn't call me until 5:30 p.m.! He was tired and didn't feel like going out, but I was welcome to come over, and he'd cook for me. After some conversation on the phone, I elected to take a rain check. I could hear him digging around in his refrigerator and freezer trying to come up with a dinner idea, and I really didn't want to go to his home. Here's the thing. Guys my age are boring. I have more energy even after all of this than most of them do! I could tell he was more of a homebody, and I just can't do boring. That's why I liked Ben and Evan, because they were younger and had some vitality.

So, I called Ben, because I was all dressed up with nowhere to go— and guess what? We went out and had a nice dinner together as friends. We also cleared the air about a few things. We both agreed it was bad timing, knowing each other only two months when I was diagnosed. He said he was devastated when I was diagnosed, which I really didn't pick up on. So, I asked why, then, did he not come to chemo and hold my hand? He said he didn't think I wanted him there. Lord: total miscommunication. It's too bad. I got sort of drunk and asked him if he wanted to try it again, and he said he couldn't go back. I understood. He has wisdom. But I'm so glad we can be friends. We were going to go to a Seattle International Film Festival flick together too, since we are both huge movie buffs.

So, yes, I got pretty drunk. I left him and went to another bar—which was a mistake—but they were so kind; they put me in a cab, and my car was safe overnight. I felt like an ass.

I should have known better than to drink and text, but I sent a text to Evan to see if he still had the girlfriend. Why, I don't know. He was poison. He replied that he was still in the relationship and said, "Have a good night; you are loved." I replied, "Bullshit," and he said, "Yes you are," to which I replied, "I love you, but I hate your fucking guts." He replied, "I know."

Then on Sunday, I had another coffee date with a different guy; that turned out to be a total bust too. He was sort of a weird conspiracy theorist and too old, and I felt nothing. He was a brainiac type too, and I could tell he wouldn't be much fun either, and I suppose he thought I wasn't up to his superior intellect.

Perhaps I am destined to be alone forever. I just don't know.

CHAPTER 25

TRYING TO MOVE BEYOND CANCER

Blog post: Monday, May 21, 2012
Feeling Pretty Good

I don't know why—well, I think I do—but I feel a bit more at peace than I have for a long time. I've been off the estrogen blocker now for six weeks, so I'm sure that has a lot to do with it. I still haven't found a job, but I continue to attempt to find something. I even went to one of those corny job fairs last week. They really aren't very stimulating, but there were a couple places I thought I should check out.

Right now, I'm sitting at the cancer center getting Herceptin. Dr. Kaplan gave me a new estrogen blocker to try out, but I won't start taking it until next week. I want to feel good this coming weekend, because I'm going glamping!

Yes, I'm going back up to my favorite place: canvas cabin #355 at Lakedale Resort on San Juan Island. I booked it for Memorial Day weekend, because I thought for sure I'd be working by now, and I can't get my deposit back now, so what the hell. I can read, think and hang out, and I am having a great new adventure Sunday. I'm going to zip line! There's a new outfit up there called Zip San Juan, and it is getting great reviews.

I wanted to do this in Hawaii but ran out of time and energy. So, it's one more thing to cross off the bucket list! Where they do it is really close to Lakedale, so they will pick me up in their van and bring me back—sweet. We'll be zipping among the huge trees there. I think it will be cool. They have all the safety equipment, so I'm not the least bit nervous—yet!

I called Dave after a few days and told him I didn't think this was going to work. I need a companion who can keep up with me! I'm not ready to sit in the easy chair and watch Netflix for a date. I like to do stuff; seriously: I'm still recovering from cancer treatment, and I have more energy than a lot of these guys. I don't and won't do boring. I guess that's part of the reason I like younger guys; they do have energy, even though some of them are incredibly immature.

Like I said before, I learned in my last group that I need to take care of me. So, I'm going glamping alone, and that's okay.

I went to Miss Rose's ukulele jam yesterday in Fremont; I had a second lesson with her Friday. I felt much more confident and held my own most of the time. Many folks in her jams are beginners, so really no one cares if you goof up. It's fun, but Lord, my hand hurt by the end! I am really having fun with this.

I finally finished the Millennium series of books, (Girl with the Dragon Tattoo, etc.) and my God, they were thrilling. I wish I could write fiction, but I just can't dream up characters like that. I would highly recommend these books to anyone who likes to read thrillers— excellent.

There's not much else to say. I am getting stronger and working out daily, getting my body ready for the next surgery: July 23. I have my girls almost lined up to come take care of me. I need someone with me for sure for two weeks. I thank all of them in advance for being such wonderful and giving friends.

So, a few days after that post, I had another coffee date with a guy named Dan. Christina set this up. He was very nice, but again, I could sense that I have way more energy. He was sweet, but I doubted he would call me again. It was okay; I had been trying really hard to look at myself more introspectively. I still hadn't found a job, and it was growing increasingly frustrating. Now, with two months until surgery, I was beginning to wonder if maybe I should just keep my feelers out but focus on taking care of myself before the next onslaught of my body.

That Monday, after my doctor's appointment, I met up with one of my former *Spokesman Review* buddies. He was in town to do some interviews for a freelance story he was working on. We had a great time together: spent some time at Dusty Strings, so he could see the beautiful instruments, and then he bought me dinner. He stayed here—in the guest room. We once were lovers, but I wouldn't go back anymore. What's the point?

I worried that I could be tempted by Evan again. He was difficult for me, as I've said before, and I couldn't stop thinking about him.

That same night, a little blessing made my week. Lakedale Resort called; the fellow on the phone sounded a little weird. He said, "Hello, Miss Ball, I see you've stayed with us before."

Hmm…I said, "Yes—twice—in canvas cabin #355."

It turned out they'd overbooked and it was Memorial Day weekend; they had a problem. He asked if I'd be willing to give up my glamp site for a deluxe room in the lodge, so I probed for the details. It was a queen-size suite, with a fireplace, deck overlooking the little lake, jetted tub and wet bar—normally $279.00 per night—and I could have it for one hundred dollars a night, which was equal to the deposit I had already made on the glamp site. So, all I would have to pay would be $12.06 when I got there. As much as I would miss my glamp site, I said, "Hell, yes!"

Two nights of luxurious, quiet bliss: children under sixteen are not allowed in the lodge! While thinking his proposition through, it occurred to me that Memorial Day weekend meant tons of kids and families in the glamp and campgrounds, so this was truly wonderful. I was so looking forward to reading, relaxing, eating nice meals, and a little pampering. That jetted tub would be nice after zip lining!

Jacci, the leader of the After Breast Cancer support group, gave us all a template to follow: a way to check in with ourselves as each of us moved on. I had started to write in it as well. I had to remind myself to be kind to myself.

I would go to San Juan Island, and I would enjoy myself. If I made a new friend: great. If I didn't, well, they would have missed out! And I would try not to worry.

I had got my girls lined up to take care of me when I would have my surgery. Laurie would take the first shift: the dreaded hospital shift. She would have to get me to the big house at 5:40 a.m., July 23. She had to drive back to

Idaho July 27, so then Taryn, also from Idaho, would take over until Colleen could get here from Alaska. I'm so lucky to have such wonderful girlfriends. It's too bad they don't live closer, but then of course, it was my choice to move here.

I really can't go anywhere else now either, because of all of this medical stuff. So, I shall make the best of it. Besides, I don't know where I'd go.

Blog post: Thursday, May 31, 2012
Time is Flying

I had a wonderful time on San Juan Island—with perfect weather. Little blessings do happen sometimes, yes? Seriously, the lodge room they gave me did indeed have a jetted tub, deck overlooking the lake, fireplace, wet bar with fridge, and a wonderful bed. And it was quiet! So, I was not glamping: I was in the lap of luxury! I could hear kids shrieking from the glamp and campgrounds, and I was so glad I wasn't there!

The ferries were so full going over Saturday that I didn't get into Friday Harbor until 6:00 p.m. I went to a new place (since last year), called Cask and Schooner, and had a wonderful dinner of risotto with scallops and a couple glasses of wine. But as I thought about it, if I were to leave Monday as planned, I'd have to be in the ferry holding area by just after 8:00 a.m., giving me only one full day on the island. So, I talked to the boys at the front desk, and yes, I could stay an extra night at the same price! I checked in with the Wiggle Room (where Miss Abbey was having her own little doggie weekend), and they said no problem, so I stayed until Tuesday morning and avoided the crowds. I'm so glad I did.

Sunday morning I went to town to Pelindaba Lavender, the store that sells all of the lavender products from the farm of the same name on the island. I love their stuff! I bought several gifts and some lotion, tea, foot soak, and dry lavender for me. I hit it off with the very nice lady, Jacke, who was working there. She was very interested in my story, as her dear friend has been dealing with cancer. We ended up having dinner together that night and exchanged contact information. She grew up on the island, moved off for some time, and plans to stay now—just a really neat person. We ate at a place called The Downrigger with a great view of the harbor but just okay food.

Sunday afternoon was my great zip lining adventure with Zip San Juan. At first I thought, oh Lord, what have I gotten myself into now, but I'm sold! I want to do it again—everywhere! It's so much fun and such an adrenaline rush. This company has a forty-acre playground, with several lines in a pattern that brings you back to where you started.

They start with a baby run so you get used to the gear and how to steer (sort of). I never felt unsafe. Then you hike a little ways to the first one, which was pretty high. I stood there for a few minutes, sucked in some air, then sat down in my harness, and off I went. It was great! You go through several runs, and each one is a little different; the last one is the longest—about 630 feet—and you fly over a pretty pond. The only part I didn't like was having to walk over one of those hanging bridges. You are still harnessed up, but it just freaked me out—I would have preferred just flying! So, I have another first under my belt.

I spent Monday exploring the two former military camps on the island and learning about the Pig War, which is a war that never really happened. It all started in 1859, because both the British and the United States claimed the San Juan Islands due to a boundary dispute. An American settler shot a boar that belonged to a British guy, because it was foraging in his garden. Well, tensions rose, and soon, both countries had established camps on opposite sides of the island and prepared for war. But they eventually chilled out; in fact, the two camps were socializing with each other before it all wound down in 1872.

Both former camps are now national parks, and it's really a very interesting, weird piece of history that largely was ignored because the Civil War was going on at the same time, so no one on the east coast even knew about it. A German arbitrator came in, and as we know, the islands were granted to the United States. Both camps were nice, but the English clearly had a more protected and scenic site. I ended up hiking quite a bit, so I was pooped. But I went back to Lakedale, rented a paddle boat for half an hour, and paddled around the little lake before taking a relaxing bath and then going to dinner at The Place, another culinary delight. This time, I had a black bean ravioli with large shrimp, cilantro, and salsa—it was splendid. There, I met a nice couple from Seattle, Katherine and Mike, and had a nice conversation with them.

I got home Tuesday and had just a little time to get Abbey, clean up, and then meet my sister Cheryle and my brother-in-law Jerry at a restaurant by the airport for an early dinner. They were heading back to Alaska after a long weekend with his sister and her husband in Shelton, across Puget Sound from me. It was so great to see them.

Today, I'm feeling a little lost. I still haven't found any work—not even any calls. I am now concerned that I won't find anything, because my surgery is now less than two months away. Who is going to hire me now if I have to tell them, "Oh by the way, I have to take two to three weeks off soon."

Maybe this is God's way of making me take time to figure some things out. I have so much work to do on getting my head right again after all of this. I need to get to a point to where I'm okay with the lady in the mirror.

I'm reading a book that was recommended by both our group leader in my After Breast Cancer class and my therapist. It's called Crucial Conversations. I hope to gain some wisdom from it.

I don't have much going on the next few days, so I guess I'll keep scoping out jobs and reading. The weather isn't the greatest today nor will it be tomorrow, so it's a good time to work on myself.

I continue to get physically stronger. I was surprised how well I did zip lining, because you have to have your arms up holding on to the strap, so clearly my range of motion is getting better. And I went to Pilates this morning, and it felt good.

Seattle is in mourning today, too, after a mentally ill man named Ian Stawicki went nuts and shot and killed five people yesterday before taking his own life. The shootings were in the University district, then downtown, but he ended up in West Seattle where the police cornered him, and he shot himself—so awful. I could see the helicopters hovering over where they found him. It was surreal and sort of nerve wracking. What is wrong with this world? Crazy people shouldn't have guns.

I started taking the new estrogen blocker yesterday, and so far, I feel okay. Time will tell if this one makes me feel bad. If that happens, Dr. Kaplan said to stop taking them and call him, which is exactly what I'll do.

Clearly, I can't take estrogen blockers. By Friday of that week, I was crying all the time and thinking all the bad stuff I was trying to not think about: the hopelessness, the loneliness, and the beating myself up for not being better. The tapes started playing—you know: old stuff that hangs on. My worst tapes are my dad telling me I'd never amount to anything, my ex-husband telling me I wasn't good at anything, and my son telling me more than once how dumb I am. I can't let them do this to me anymore.

Estrogen suppressants—my ass; I won't take them anymore...period. I called Kaplan's office and talked to nurse Steph, who talked to him, and he said to stop—no shit. I didn't want to live my life feeling like I had twenty-four-hour PMS. I'd rather take the risk: five percent wasn't that much, and quality of life was far more important to me. I'd like to feel good about myself as long as I'm alive.

CHAPTER 26

SOME SUMMER FUN BEFORE SURGERY

Blog post: Monday, June 11, 2012
Sunshine!

Wow, the sun is out today, and it feels so good! I had Herceptin today, and of course, I saw Dr. Kaplan. I did indeed try another estrogen blocker and quit taking it, too, after three days. Jesus, I had a nightmare I was in some huge house under lock and key, because there were bad guys trying to get in. No one would tell me exactly what was going on, but it involved espionage. I credit that to the fact that I had recently finished the Millennium series of books.

Anyway, in the dream, I was in my bedroom in this mansion, and I saw a shadowy figure in the window, and I'm not kidding, it was the Grim Reaper. Of course, I couldn't scream—like it happens with so many people and bad dreams—but then, when I did, it was out loud: and I do mean loud! The dog started barking, and I woke up just freaked out—no more estrogen blockers.

Dr. Kaplan understands. I told him I had horrendous PMS when I did have menses, and those damn pills made me feel like I have 24-7 PMS. It's okay. I've done everything else to stave off the cancer. So, all in all, I'm doing famously, and my reconstructive surgery is six weeks from today! I can't wait to get a new boob!

All my girls are lined up now. Colleen made her reservations yesterday, so, in order: I'll have Laurie, Taryn, and then Colleen coming to be my nurses. At the tail end of Colleen's stay, we're going to Aerosmith at the Tacoma Dome! Nothing can slow this girl down.

I'm feeling so hopeful—Lord knows why. I still haven't found a real job, but with the advice, inspiration and support of a few other writer friends, I'm dipping my toe into serious freelancing. So, we'll see how it goes.

And I have big, great news! Love and smooches to my dear Jill and Viv, aka WaveJourney.com: a fabulous travel web site. They are leaving for Europe Friday and won't be back until August 10 (I know: brats!). A couple years ago, they went on a sailing adventure on the Schooner Zodiac out of Bellingham and wrote about it for Wave. They were invited to come back and write about an upcoming wine cruise through the San Juans (one of my favorite places!), and of course, they can't go, because they'll be in Europe. So, they asked the first mate if another writer could come in their place, and guess who that is—me! Yay! I'm so psyched! I will be a guest, for free, and write a story for Wave Journey. I'm also hoping to pitch it to perhaps a wine magazine or a Northwest Mag. Viv said the food is great too. They feed us three nice meals a day, plus snacks and wine. I'll have a berth for accommodations, but Viv said it's private when I pull my little curtain. Hell, if there's a cute guy in another berth nearby—one can only hope! I'm so bad.

And I will get to learn to sail. Guests take turns doing various jobs on the ship. Check it out at SchoonerZodiac.com. I'm just beside myself. So, I'll drive up to Bellingham the twenty-seventh, and we sail the twenty-eighth in the morning, returning Sunday, July 1. Surgery is July 23.

I'm having a barbecue this Saturday for my friends here, and I'm looking forward to it. I haven't had the energy to entertain for quite some time, so it's time.

The weekend of June 23 is Ukefest at Dusty Strings, and I'm excited about that too. I am signed up for two workshops, and of course, Sunga's jam—she's my new teacher. Oh my God, I learned to do some fancy picking at my last lesson, and I really get it! And I can do several chords without looking at my hands.

I feel alive again! That's it —as Pearl Jam sings: "Oh, oh, oh, I'm still alive!" Eddie, take me away!

At the helm of the Schooner Zodiac, a 160-foot sailboat.
This was such a wonderful opportunity before my reconstruction.

Blog post: Tuesday, June 19, 2012
Fear, Anxiety, and Hair

I had a haircut today. It's pretty amazing, but it needed some shaping, as it was getting sort of shaggy in places. I made an appointment for early August to shape it up again. It's encouraging how fast it's growing back.

I've had a rough couple of days. I got all the paperwork in the mail from the plastic surgeon, Dr. Isik, regarding my reconstruction, which is coming up fast. I read every word and sort of got freaked out. Of course, this stuff always includes something to the effect that the worst-case scenario is death. Super! (Note: sarcasm).

I go in four weeks from yesterday for the first procedure, which is done in-office. This is the delay I talked about earlier. What it boils down to is cutting me open in the abdominal area and tying off blood vessels that are no larger than the point of a pen—to force more blood into the area. I just can't even imagine how the hell he does this. So, I'm under anesthesia for that one and come home the same day.

Then, on the twenty-third is the TRAM flap itself. I was of the impression that they actually remove the tissue from the belly and move it up to create the new breast, but I was wrong. That's the magic of it all: Dr. Isik will just kind of scoot it up, "it" being a vertical mass of muscle and fat. Therefore, the blood supply is never disrupted. It's so amazing what they can do, but I'm getting freaked, because it's a five-hour operation and again, anesthesia. I've never not woken up before, but you never know.

Adding to my anxiety is the fact that Taylor is now in Colorado to fight the wildfires there, since there's no action in Idaho. He's fine—I just talked to him today, and they are basically patrolling right now to check for smoke or new fires. I mean, they are newbies, so I can't imagine they'll throw them into some sort of disco inferno. But it still makes me nervous. Oh shit, he just sent me a text: they just got dispatched. Sweet Jesus, keep my boy safe.

So, I have been very unproductive the past two days. I am seeing Dr. Isik Friday morning—just to talk and get all my nitty-gritty questions I have hopefully answered. There's a lot of info in the packet they sent that I can't even begin to describe. You can Google Dr. Frank Isik and the TRAM flap if you want the medical details. It is fascinating.

Meantime, I did have a lovely barbecue Saturday night with the usual suspects: Jim, Mira, Christina, and her sweetie, Don. I invited more people, but it's always something I guess. It kind of hurt my feelings, because I busted my ass to make everything perfect, and I won't be entertaining again anytime soon. But the five of us had a grand time!

Ukefest is this weekend; I'll be going to a concert and participating in two workshops and a jam. Then, next Wednesday, I'll drive up to Bellingham, spend the night there, and then board the Schooner Zodiac for my four-day San Juan Island Cruise on assignment for Wave Journey—which I'm really looking forward to. It will be a lovely break before all medical hell breaks loose again.

CHAPTER 27

EVAN IS BACK IN MY LIFE

June 9, 2012

What can I say? I'm hopelessly in love with this man. Like a dumb shit, I drank a little too much one night and called him. At this point, I hadn't seen him in ten weeks. He didn't answer his phone, so I just hung up quickly. Much to my shock and almost horror, he called right back.

Small talk: yes, he still had the girlfriend, and he was happy to hear from me. He'd call me soon, and we'd have lunch and catch up.

Three days later, I was just about to head home after seeing a movie at the Seattle International Film Festival, which was extremely good and was ironically about a love affair between an older woman and younger man: art imitating my life.

After the movie, I had some pizza and two glasses of wine at a place where happy hour is from 3:00 p.m. until closing. I was just about to head onto the freeway, and he sent me a text: "How are you?" Fine, I say, and I add that I'm heading home from a film.

Would I like to visit? I knew what was up, and I headed toward his neighborhood on autopilot.

He said he was looking forward to seeing me.

I arrive at his apartment and told him he scared me the last time I saw him. He said he was in a bad place then, and he scared a lot of people. He was very alert and said he was backing off from activism and politics to focus on his own life—which is a good thing. And he's broke: a bad thing. I asked about the girlfriend, and while she's still around, he said if everything were great, I wouldn't be there.

We made love. I couldn't help myself. It had been forever: I mean, the last time I had sex was with him, and that was the beginning of March, and now it's well into June. It was tender and beautiful. What shocked me the most was that my prosthetic was really hurting. (I still had my bra on—no one has seen the big ugly except my doctor, my sister, and one gal pal) I asked him if he'd mind if I took it off—if he'd be too grossed out—and he was so wonderful about it. I took it off; he didn't recoil in horror: far from it. He said I was beautiful; and I couldn't help it; and soon it will be fixed—not to worry. The moment I took my bra off, I started to cry: tears just poured out, and I don't know why—relief, acceptance—it all just came out. It felt so good to hold him close, skin to skin.

He'll never be my "man," I think I know this, but I can always hope. The age difference has us in a different place, I think, but God knows—He really does—that I love this man so much, no matter how much he hurts me. I can't help myself. He's so beautiful in my eyes.

Although invited, he didn't come to my barbecue a week later. I had told him to bring his sister. I was really hoping they both would come, but by late in the afternoon the day of the barbecue, I still hadn't received an RSVP, so I had sent him a text. He was really down, broke, and tired from staying up half the night trying to protect the building from thugs. I was pretty worried about him.

On the following Monday, he sent me a text and said he was working at a little place in Pike Place Market where he did reflexology sometimes, and he'd trade me a full body massage for food. That sounded good to me. I used the rest of the salmon from the barbecue to make him a salmon salad sandwich, and then I put a big chunk of focaccia bread, the last piece of Mira's fabulous but very filling apple pie, a bottle of water, a beer, and some chocolates in a bag. Lord knows I didn't need all those fattening leftovers around, and he is so not fat at all! I love his body and wish mine were normal.

When I got there, he was doing a henna tattoo then reflexology on a lady who was there with her husband. They were visiting from Florida and were very cool indeed. The husband kept saying how laid back Seattle was compared to South Beach, Florida, and she kept talking about how all the women had fake lips and boobs and everything. Okay, so yes, I was getting reconstruction, but it wasn't like a boob job just for kicks!

Anyway, Evan got done with the nice lady, and it was just the two of us. He ate the sandwich and felt much better. He'd only had a banana all day. That's just not good.

The lady that owned the business was away that week, so he got the gig, which is great, as he gets half of whatever the place brings in. Now, he wasn't a licensed massage therapist, but he was pretty good. He needed to work on pressure points and identifying pain and how to relieve it, but when he worked on my legs and feet (he was so good at feet), it felt great. We started with me face up, so when I flipped over, he worked on my back. Pretty soon, he was massaging my thighs and my buttocks—hmm…hardly standard for a massage.

It felt so good. He was tired from working on me; I was fine too. I flipped over, and we started making out and ended up making love on the massage table, and it was fabulous, erotic, exciting, and passionate.

I was reading Carole King's bio, and she talked about the lyrics to one of the first big hits she wrote with her ex-husband and collaborator, Gerry Goffin: a song called "Chains." It goes: "Chains, my baby's got me locked up in chains, and they ain't the kind that you can see—wo-oh, these chains of love got a hold on me."

King goes on to say that the metaphor is about being so deeply in love that all you can think of is the object of your desire, and even as you wish you could stop being obsessed with that person, you spend every sleeping moment dreaming about the one you love and every waking moment praying that he or she feels the same about you. That's how I felt about Evan. It was insane. I'm twenty years older than he is, he had no money and didn't always treat me right, but I would have loved to be the object of his desire as much as he was mine. I loved him and would grow old with him in a New York minute if he'd have considered it. I'd have treated him right. I'd have been a much better partner this time.

He told me he doesn't think he's really been in love. I have. I loved my husband dearly for a long time until we just grew apart. I also loved one other in my life, very deeply, and then, Evan.

He also said he and the girlfriend had broken up. I hated being his in-between-girlfriends girlfriend, but I guess that is what I was. I knew I deserved better. But love makes you do funny things; and I trusted him.

We got together again a week later. I needed to borrow a sleeping bag for my upcoming sailing adventure. I told him I'd make him dinner. I picked him up and thought, my goodness, that's a huge sleeping bag. It turned out that he had brought his laundry in a duffle bag to do at my place. I did not do his laundry! But in typical male fashion, he threw colors in with whites and just basically threw it back into the duffle bag when it was dry. Men are weird. We had a nice dinner (nothing fancy) and made love again—twice: both were fantastic, sweaty, and hot. We had such incredible chemistry.

As it would turn out, I didn't see him again before my reconstructive surgery, so that day, June 24, would be the last time we made love for a while—maybe ever for all I knew, because he was back with the girlfriend.

CHAPTER 28

RECONSTRUCTION - PART ONE

Blog post: Thursday, July 5, 2012
Calm before the Storm

Actually, the weather was absolutely perfect today, and it will be for the foreseeable future. It's interesting how seventy degrees feels like one hundred in Seattle! Everyone is out walking, riding bikes, and sunning themselves. It's glorious. I'm happy it's sunny, because I'm getting nervous about my upcoming surgery. Gloomy weather right now would really put me in a funk.

I'm back from my wonderful San Juan Island wine cruise, and I am still working on the story. So much happened it's hard to get it all down. It was the best short vacation I've ever had. Depression set in almost immediately when I returned to the reality of my apartment and upcoming doctors' appointments.

It's hard to explain, but I felt like I had a family again on the boat. With only twelve crew and eighteen passengers—in close quarters— you become pretty good pals. And since I haven't had a job in a while, the fact that it was a learning and working cruise made it feel like I had a purpose. I hate not feeling useful.

So, I'm not a bad-ass sailor—yet, but it sure was cool being a part of it. I won't go into the details here: when the story is done, I'll link it to Facebook, but if you're not on Facebook, it will be on WaveJourney. com for sure within a week or so.

I did have a wonderful little victory this week. I had an essay published in High Country News, a magazine in Colorado, and they are actually paying me! So, it's my first published, paid magazine piece. I hesitate to talk about it too much, because it's about my perspective as a mother whose son is fighting the firestorm in Colorado. Taylor rarely, if ever, reads my blog, so I am talking about it here. He doesn't like me talking about him, but if he does stumble upon it, I think he'll be pleased. It's at hcn.org under "Writers on the Range," and it's called: "A Different Voice on the Phone."

I realized it was there as I was walking back to get my Herceptin treatment Tuesday, and my blood pressure shot up! It was kind of funny. (My blood pressure is really good, by the way: usually on the low side.)

My white blood count is still low, and that's probably why I was so exhausted when I got back from the cruise. Well, that and the cook rang the breakfast bell at 7:00 a.m., and we were at it all day: either sailing or going onshore to taste wine and then drinking wine and eating into the night—tough gig, right? I even jammed on uke with two of the crew who brought their ukes! They were brothers (both in their twenties), seasoned sailors, and little darlings.

So next week, I see my original breast surgeon for a checkup, then I have my pre-op with Dr. Isik on the eleventh. The first procedure, the "delay," is July 16. My dear Jim, my friend forever in Tacoma, is going to take me to that appointment and bring me home, because they will knock me out. I don't have to stay in the hospital for that one. Then on the twenty-first, Laurie arrives for the first nurse shift. I've made a reservation for brunch at Book Bindery (my fave) for Sunday, to show her my appreciation and eat a nice meal in case I don't wake up from the big one on the twenty-third!

I am exercising, cleaning, organizing, writing—just trying to accomplish as much as I can before I have to lie low. I did not gain any weight on the boat, because we were pretty active when we weren't eating or drinking! I dread being down for the count, but I look forward to the result and getting back to normal: normal with scars. My friend

Sarah says they will be scars I should be proud of. That's a tough one to grasp right now.

Blog post: Thursday, July 12, 2012
A Little Pity Party

I apologize to those who saw my Facebook post I put up briefly last night before I took it down. But it seems it still lived somewhere, because I had several responses. A scary pre-op appointment and three-fourths of a bottle of wine (among other things) sent me into a major funk. I'm sorry.

I did see Dr. Beatty, my breast surgeon, Monday, and it was great to see him. He's so caring and supportive. He was very reassuring about the reconstructive surgery. He said I'm in excellent hands with Dr. Isik, and I will wake up—not to worry. Even after reconstruction, I may never have normal feeling in my left breast again, which is a bummer. I basically have no feeling there from nerve damage.

I'm not so worried about the delay procedure this coming Monday. It's going to be a breeze compared to the twenty-third. It will just be a small incision: enough for Dr. Isik to ligate some blood vessels. But I'll be goofy all day from the drugs. The twenty-third is a different story.

When I had my mastectomy, I had to deal with that drain for what seemed like forever. It sort of looks like a hand grenade, and it fills up with God knows what that comes out of your body: fluid you don't want building up. My sister Cheryle knew how much I hated that thing—mainly because it hurt. Well, after this surgery, I get the thrill of not one, but two drains and this other device that will be hanging out of me so I can dose myself with pain med. I can't OD: it's designed to only allow you to dose once an hour. I do get to stay in the hospital a day or two, but I'll be coming home with all of this crap hanging out of me, and it just upsets me so much—that and being under anesthesia for six hours.

So, I sort of lost it. But I'm better today after taking a nap, and I'm basically not going anywhere. I wrote a story today for my old employer, and I am getting paid out of their not-so-lucrative freelance budget.

The story is upsetting to me too. It's a follow up about an aspiring figure skater who has real potential. The kicker is—and this isn't in the story to save the girl from ridicule at school—her family has recently become homeless. She just won a competition in Everett and has serious Olympic aspirations. She is very good. But it just pisses me off—the situation. Her mom, who is a single mom, lost her job two years ago after twenty-three years with the same company, and things are just unraveling.

Then, a dear friend of mine lost her job this week—another professional just like me. I am beginning to wonder what the hell is happening to this country. I don't want to get into politics, but I'm having a hard time with the state of the economy and how it is ruining people's lives. I'm sure as hell not voting for Romney; he won't give a rat's ass about people like me, but I'm losing faith in Obama—even though I admire him greatly.

Once I'm all better and over with all of my cancer treatments and surgeries, I'm beginning to wonder if I'll ever have a real job again. The odds aren't good for folks my age. But I still continue to apply for jobs, even if no one responds, so I can continue to be honest in receiving my unemployment. Oh, yeah, and those rat bastards at the Department of Labor sent me a letter (which came yesterday), adding to my anger and frustration. They are going to audit me next week to be sure I really am looking for work.

Let me at them. I've got all the proof—bastards.

So, I think freelancing and minding my investments are my best options right now, especially since I will require four to six weeks to recover from the surgery.

It's looking hopeful that NW Yachting is going to pick up my story on the Schooner Zodiac adventure too, so I picked up a hard copy of the magazine yesterday at a local marina shop. It's sort of like a big tabloid: with lots and lots of ads for boats of all kinds for sale. I'm intrigued now with the idea of just buying a boat I can live on, figuring out where to moor it, and writing and being at peace someday. It *doesn't seem like the normal American dream is going to happen to me—whatever that normal is—so, why not? I can sail away.*

Blog post: Monday, July 16, 2012
This Was an Easy One

Had the delay procedure this morning, and I'm doing fine—albeit, a little woozy from pain killers. This was done in the small OR at the Polyclinic where Dr. Isik has his practice. Next Monday, I'll be in the big house (as I like to call it), aka Swedish Hospital on Broadway, where I had all my other surgeries.

It hurt when the anesthesiologist first started to push the night-night stuff into me, then I heard them saying my name, and it was over. My first thought was, oh my God, I overslept and missed it!

I've got gauze and Steri-Strips over the two incisions. I can take the gauze off tomorrow. Jim is here, and I'm just taking it easy.

This is funny: It's a beautiful day, so after I got up from a nap, we were sitting outside eating tuna sandwiches. My cute neighbor came by with her new baby, so I got up to coo over the baby. Well, Jim was too busy looking at the cute neighbor (she is adorable—a slim little thing that doesn't even look like she just had a baby), and while he was gawking, Abbey made off with half of his sandwich! It serves him right! Don't be too concerned; he was on his second sandwich. So, Abbey scored big time. Good dog!

Okay, I'm lying low but just wanted to report that I lived.

The rest of that week would prove to be difficult. I was in much more pain than I expected, so I was taking painkillers, which of course helped with the pain, but they really interfered with my sleep. I felt like I hadn't really slept all week. Add to that: stocking up on groceries for my girls and just continuing to get my shit together—I was more than a little overwhelmed.

I had talked to Evan on the phone since I returned from my sailing trip, but I hadn't seen him. I would have been so happy if he had come to see me in the hospital—just to hold my hand.

CHAPTER 29

BOOTY CALL

So, where the hell *was* Evan during all of this? He didn't show up at the hospital to hold my hand as I had hoped, and he certainly didn't send flowers.

I had been home from the hospital all of eleven hours when my cell phone rang. I thought it was odd that it was ringing at 2:00 a.m., because I had set it for 1:00 a.m. to take my pain pill, and I'd only been to sleep for another hour.

I looked at the caller ID and saw his name. What? I was so out of it—I just sort of answered, "What?"

Here was his nicey voice, "Hello Linda, this is Evan." Yeah, so? Turned out he'd been at a friend's house in West Seattle and didn't realize the bus had quit running, so he was stranded in West Seattle. I said, "I just got out of the hospital."

The light dawned: "Oh, you must be exhausted," he said, genuinely surprised. The fucker forgot when my surgery was. I just basically mumbled, and we hung up.

Seriously…seriously? Oh, he did say he'd come see me soon.

I suppose he expected me to come and get him and either crash here or have me take him back downtown. I can only surmise that he was possibly at the on-and-off girlfriend's house, who also lived in West Seattle, or with some other friend. Well, then why didn't he go back to her house if that was where he was? Perhaps she dumped his ass again. Or why wouldn't he go back to his buddy's house? I couldn't believe it.

This time, I was so deeply disappointed in him, I had changed the way I saw him. He needed to grow up and think of others and how they felt. It wasn't all about him.

He sent me a text August 11 that simply said hi. Hi—really? I replied that I lived but was still recovering. I should have added, "Thanks for asking, dick head."

CHAPTER 30

RECONSTRUCTION - PART 2

Blog post: Monday, August 6, 2012
Worse than Childbirth

Now that it's over, I think I'm going to be extremely happy I made the decision I did. But I'm still extremely tired and sore from the TRAM flap. If I had known how much pain I would be in, I might have chickened out. I told Taylor I think I'd rather have given birth to him ten times over.

The days leading up to the surgery were the calm before the storm. I was sore from the delay procedure, but when Laurie arrived for first shift as my nurse Saturday night, we had a little wine and visited, then the next day had brunch at Book Bindery, followed by a ride on the Great Seattle Wheel on Pier 57—a new feature to the Emerald City.

I hardly slept. I was totally awake by 3:00 a.m. and just gave up. We were at the hospital right on time: at 5:40 a.m.—"O'dark hundred." Being early on the OR schedule, there was no waiting—unlike with my mastectomy where I was in the holding area a grueling six hours. It was frightening moving along so quickly. When it was time to say goodbye to Laurie, I wasn't ready. This time while waiting to be conked out, I was regaling the anesthesiologist and staff with the story of my emergency appendectomy during the time I was going through chemo, then I was in recovery. It's funny how they always shut me up.

Oh, this time I didn't have the cute anesthesiologist: I had a female. Before I went on my sailing adventure, I decided to splurge on eye lash extensions, knowing I wouldn't have much bathroom time on the boat. They look so pretty, and you don't need mascara! I had a fill (they get spruced up) five days before surgery, hoping to get cutie-pie again for my anesthesiologist. No such luck, in fact it was a nice lady anesthesiologist, who asked me if I had on mascara, and I said no. Then she asked if they were my real eyelashes, and I said, "Sort of." I told her they were extensions, and that they were attached to my real eye lashes. That's when I learned they tape your eyes shut during surgery! She said it could pull off my extensions, and she just wanted to warn me. Shit. But, as it turned out, they were fine, and when Laurie saw me, she told me my eyelashes survived! Yay!

I was in recovery for two hours. I couldn't feel the pain, as I still had tons of drugs in me—plus a catheter, IV, and three drains. Laurie finally got to see me when they took me to my room on the eleventh floor, and she told me Dr. Isik said it went very well, but it took a little longer than expected, because the tissue was harder than he anticipated. Ha— Pilates! It was 3:00 p.m.

I wasn't really hungry, so after a while I had some Jell-O and vanilla wafers. Laurie took off to go take care of sweet Abbey and to have dinner with another friend of hers who was in Seattle visiting from New York. I was happy she had someone else to entertain her. Mira came to see me from 8:00 p.m. until 9:00 p.m., and we laughed, and she and Nurse Bonnie were marveling about how good I looked. Bonnie said most people have a gray pallor right out of surgery, and she was stunned that I had color in my face. Note: I had not slipped into any makeup! Anyway, Mira said the funniest thing: she said, "Surgery becomes you." I laughed until it was hurting, and I had to quit!

One hour later, all hell broke loose. All the big drugs must have worn off, because I was in excruciating pain. It took Bonnie until 11:30 p.m. to get me comfortable. I was shaking, crying, and wishing I'd just die.

I said to her, "How can I go home tomorrow? I can hardly move?"

She was a tough bird. She said by golly, I have patient's rights, and if I don't want to go home Tuesday, I don't have to. I stayed.

Dr. Isik came in Tuesday morning, and I told him I couldn't possibly go home and have Laurie dealing with this pile of mush that can't even move, and he was fine with that. They took my catheter out, which meant I was going to have to get up to go to the bathroom. It was so much effort. Then, I couldn't sit low enough to reach it, so they had to bring in a high-rise toilet. My first walk to the nurses' station and back was total hell. I didn't think I'd make it. What had I done?

Much to my amazement, by Wednesday morning, not only was I able to go the regular toilet by myself, I could also walk a short distance. Bonnie had gone home early in the morning, and I had another wonderful nurse, Megan, most of Tuesday. But then dipshit Trang came back (I had her in the beginning), and I was getting pissed. She was the most inept nurse ever: totally stupid. I had snapped at her more than once about making me wait for my pain medication. I said to her, "I don't think you realize how much pain I'm in: this is not make-believe." Then, I waited an hour to get a diet Sierra Mist and chicken noodle soup (Campbell's sucky soup), and I was ready to get out of there. I was home by 3:00 p.m. and felt better already in my own digs. Abbey was thrilled to see me, but we had to be very careful to keep her from jumping on my belly. I think she understood something was up with mom—what, she wasn't sure, but she's been a really good girl.

All was pretty quiet for the next forty-eight hours. I slept a lot. Laurie was fine—she was confident enough to go here and there in her car, but she stayed close to home after I got out of the hospital. So Thursday, Taryn arrived for shift number two. Both would stay that night. In advance, I had gone to one of those places where you put dinners together ahead of time and freeze them, so I had a nice cod in, I think, some sort of lemon sauce, which they prepared along with a really good salad, and Taryn brought some awesome lemon bread from a bakery in Idaho.

Now, let me tell you, pain killers—any kind—have one really nasty side effect: constipation. I had been taking a stool softener daily, but it was Thursday now, and I hadn't moved the earth since Sunday. I was miserable. When the girls ran out to the store, they got me some Milk of Magnesia, which the doc said was fine. I swigged a capful and was off to the bathroom. Once again, I wanted to die. I didn't realize it, but I was in there an hour and forty-five minutes—screaming, moaning, and begging for mercy—while they held dinner. I know they were cracking up, but it wasn't funny. So, finally I yelled for whoever was brave enough to crack open the bathroom door and hand me my medical marijuana, because it helps move things too. Taryn dashed in and delivered the goods. In retrospect, it was hilarious. She came back again (for what, I've forgotten), but she swears she got a second-hand high. It's amazing the bathroom didn't explode.

Suffice it to say, I was exhausted, but I did enjoy my dinner. I was in bed not too much later. Then, I had a nightmare and woke up screaming, and both of them came running into my bedroom. A few hours later, I thought Abbey was crying, so everyone got up again. Lord, I have such wonderful friends.

Laurie left bright and early, so now Taryn had to deal with me on her own.

Taryn is a small-town girl, so I was amazed when she said she'd come to the big city to take care of me. So, she didn't go anywhere for days—except to walk Abbey! Let me digress for a moment to Abbey. She's so funny. At first, she wouldn't walk with Laurie. She'd plant her ass on the sidewalk and refuse to move. Momma wasn't there. But soon, she realized if she wanted to be walked, she didn't have much of a choice. Then, Taryn arrives—same drill: she digs her heels in and won't budge. It was so funny; finally, Taryn had to run sort of in place to get her moving, then Abbey would go! I can only imagine what that looked like outside. I took her for a very short walk today, and she was very happy, although I walk at a snail's pace. So, now she needed to get ready for Colleen. If she wants a serious walk, I'm not there yet. She's so damn spoiled! It turned out, she walked just fine for Colleen, because I think she remembers Col, since she is down here a few times each year.

By Sunday, Taryn's dad (Carl), step-mom (Shelley), and half brother, Rick, were able to come and rescue her and take her to lunch and out and about a bit in West Seattle. They came in and visited with me on both ends. What a nice couple, and I had never met Rick; he's a neat kid. He's twenty-three and was in a band, so I asked him if he was the rock star, and he looked at me sort of hesitantly and shrugged and said, sure!

The next day, I was thrilled, because I got my drains out: all three of them! The C drain, out the right side of my abdomen, filled the most, but it was well below 30ml in a twenty-four-hour period. So they were only in a week—compared to three weeks with my mastectomy drain, *which I thought was interesting, because this was a much more invasive procedure. With no icky stuff hanging out of me, Taryn and I were able to enjoy a nice dinner at a West Seattle place called Blackboard Bistro that evening. I was so happy to get out.*

In addition to the obvious pain from my wounds, my back hurt like a "mo-fo." I've had lower back problems anyway, but walking with a slight stoop from my belly hurting made it worse. Much to my amazement, Naomi, the best massage therapist I've found here, makes house calls! She came with her table to my home and massaged the hell out of my back, relieving a great deal of pressure and pain. I plan to go to her again—soon. It really, really helped. By mid-week I was able to see Dr. Isik, and he was thrilled with my progress. That was ten days out. He took off the Steri-Strips and any remaining stitches and said he'd see me in a month—a month? But as I write this, none of my guts have fallen out!

Dr. Isik told me to keep paper tape over my abdominal incision 24–7, changing it when I showered, and it would greatly reduce scarring. Who knew? As far as the breast incisions, he said one positive to radiation is that the tissue won't scar. Again, who knew? I feel like the bride of Frankenstein right now, but it will be awesome when I'm all healed.

When Taryn and I went to get my drains out, one of the nurses who had this procedure years ago showed us her boobs and her belly, and we were duly impressed! But it was so funny to suddenly be flashed by this woman we didn't know. We told Dr. Isik about it, and he smiled and said, "Everybody has seen her boobs but me." He didn't do her surgery, because this was before she knew him, so it was really funny!

Taryn rolled out Thursday, and Colleen arrived late that night from Anchorage. She got the easier shift, because I'm able now to do more for myself, but I do get tired easily, and I still sleep a lot. We did make it to a good vantage point Friday to see the Blue Angels perform in day one of their "Seafair" performances, and as usual, they were breathtaking. We totally lucked out finding a parking place and then ending up at this same little spot I found two years ago. Saturday night, we had dinner at the wonderful Book Bindery. I seem to take all my out-of-town guests there! It's so damn good! We shared a bottle of wine—which I hadn't done in a while—and boy, did I sleep that night. Then, I had to take a nap and go to bed early the next night—oh boy.

Hopefully, I will have more strength in two days, as we have tickets to see Aerosmith at the Tacoma Dome. I plan to take a good nap in the afternoon! I figure I can do this—after all, I was at the U2 concert last year one week after the appendectomy! Rock-n-roll is always a priority!

Blog post: Monday August 13, 2012
Back to Normal—Sort Of

With all my caregivers gone, I'm trying to rest up, get caught up, and pursue looking for work with more enthusiasm; although, I don't know if I could work yet. I get so darn tired. I'm three weeks post-op now. I made it to Aerosmith with Col last Wednesday night and slept in the next day. Yesterday, I made it to yet another concert: this one an earlier show, because it was at the Zoo (part of their Zootunes series), and they always start at 6:00 p.m. sharp and don't go much later than 9:00 because of neighboring homes, I imagine. So, I was home by 8:45 or so.

I saw Melissa Ethridge—one of my favorite ladies of rock. I saw her once before, years ago, before she had breast cancer. I could tell it changed her too. She's one of those artists who talks to the audience between songs, and you can actually understand her! She said she's eight years cancer free now—I figured it had been awhile; plus, her hair is long again!

So, when she opened her encore with "I Walk for Life" (which she wrote after the whole cancer thing), it was really emotional for me: tears welling up in my eyes.

I had an epiphany too. I think one of the reasons I love rock so much is that I understand the message so well. Rock and blues musicians speak to me—I get it. It's the soundtrack of my life. They express thoughts and feelings about life as I would like to.

Before "I'm The Only One" (one my favorites of hers), Melissa pointed out that we are the only ones who truly get it—about who we are. I need to take care of myself—it's my life, you know? I mean, I know this, but it's good to be reminded.

So, enough of the philosophy of rock and roll! She is a rock star—but not flashy. She opened with "Fearless Love" and "Your Little Secret" before launching into a killer blues jam. She can certainly hold her own on the axe, let me tell you.

"I Want to Come Over" was performed with a whole lot of yearning, and then she did "You Can't Always Get What You Want," doing the Stones proud—loved it.

She's funny too. Her belt broke, so her wardrobe/hair/makeup guy had to come out with a new belt or "her britches would fall down." She turned it into an amusing little dance while she strummed guitar, and he circled her putting on the new belt. She said she was helpless and hapless (?) without him!

She also applauded her male fans, saying they were the best, because it took a lot of guts to admit they were Melissa Ethridge fans! (She's gay, if you don't know.)

Of course, she did "Come to my Window." When she travels, she said people will ask her what she does, and she tells them she's an entertainer. They'll ask, "Do you play guitar?" Yes. "Do you sing?" Yes. Then she says, "You know that window song?" Ohh! They immediately know who she is.

She's got a new album coming out September 4 and did a couple of songs off of it: one called "Falling Up" that was particularly good.

The rest of my week is pretty dull. Right now, I have a massage scheduled for Thursday with Naomi again—still trying to get my back straightened out. I may also have an informational interview for a job—keep your fingers crossed.

No doctors until the last week of August. I'm going to have withdrawals! It's really scary to have the doctors' appointments thinning out—all normal...or so I hear.

CHAPTER 31

NEXT STEPS

Blog post: Sunday, August 19, 2012
Cold Turkey

Well hell, I wish the doctor had told me to wean myself off the painkillers. After my last post, they ran out, and I thought, okay, I'm done, because I didn't want to become dependent on them. I was on oxycodone: bad shit—real bad shit. I didn't leave the house for two days, and Tuesday—it was in the eighties outside—I lay on the couch, rolled up in a ball in a blanket, crying, freezing and sweating. God, it was awful.

Wednesday I had to go to Swedish to talk to the social worker about continued assistance, so I had to go out among them, which was a good thing. I took care of some other business and went to Costco too, and I felt much more human.

Sandy, the social worker, told me something I didn't know: for every hour you're under anesthesia, it takes a week to recover and get it out of your system. I was under for five hours. Tomorrow is four weeks out, so I figure another week, and I may feel like myself again, and hopefully in another two or three, I can get into some restorative yoga.

I am able to walk Abbey longer now. We went to Lincoln Park for the first time in a month, and it was a gorgeous, hot sunny day.

We just walked along the water though, as I still don't have it in me to trek through the woods. But it was wonderful.

I had another massage with Naomi—which really helps my back. What a goddess she is with her hands. My belly incision doesn't hurt so much anymore either, so I'm trying to stand in the Pilates stance when I'm standing, and I tuck my tailbone under. My new breast still hurts. It's still very swollen and bruised. I'm going to call the doc tomorrow just to make sure that's normal.

I'm also sleeping better. I was having God-awful night sweats, and now that I'm off the oxy—surprise!—the night sweats are gone. Imagine waking up every morning soaked and freezing. I can't even imagine how people get hooked on pain killers. It's awful.

But now I've been burdened with GI problems all week from going off the oxycodone. Nothing looks good to me. So, I'm forcing myself to eat a BRAT diet (bananas, rice, applesauce, and toast), and it's working. As much as I know I need fruits and veggies again—which I love—it's hard right now. I did eat some cucumber and tomato, and today I had some cantaloupe, banana, and blueberries. Consequently, I've lost weight! Yay!

But yesterday was a great day. I met up with my old pal from the Coeur d'Alene Press days: Tyler Wilson, and his wife Angie, and their little girl Marion—along with some other people I didn't know—and had a lovely visit in Sodo before they went to a Mariner's game. Tyler is a great guy. Then, I went to a dive bar called Linda's Tavern, of all things, for Linda's Fest, to catch a new band, "Walking Papers," and I was blown away! I even met the drummer and on bass: the one and only Duff McKagan, formerly of Guns n' Roses! I was so stoked! They were totally killer. The lead singer/guitarist, Jeff Angell, is awesome. The drummer, Barrett Martin, and Angell are the main guys; who knows if Duff will stay with them, but I was right in front! I love being able to see all the details, setting up, plugging stuff in, and the set list. It electrifies me.

Today I went to a uke jam and had fun as usual. I've been working on "Norwegian Wood," by the Beatles, for weeks and finally got the lick down. It's a hard one. We didn't do it at the jam, but I'm enjoying it as part of my repertoire. I watched Duff and Jeff very closely last night: their hands on the frets, their strumming, and plucking patterns. Geez—I'll never be a rock star, but I sure do admire the talent. I know it's only rock and roll, but dammit, I love it!

Taylor is coming over for a couple of days, and then I'm taking off again in a week for a couple of nights on Whidbey Island. I haven't been there in ages. I found a quaint pet-friendly Inn in Coupeville, so I'm taking Miss Abbey on a little adventure. I'm going to scout around. I figure if I don't find a job here by the time all my cancer care is over, I might be outa here. I don't know. I love Seattle, but Whidbey is close enough, so if I wanted to go to a show or something, I could still do it. God knows I love the San Juans, but that's quite a commute. I need to find a place where I can live cheaper, and I want to stay near the water.

I wouldn't get to see Taylor much, because he came over with friends, including a new love interest, but I did still get to see him and hug him. I hadn't seen him since Christmas! He had finished firefighting school then went straight to work for the Dept. of Lands. It had been a hell of a summer for wildfires, so he'd been super busy. I hoped when the job ended in October he could come over and just spend time with me for our birthdays, maybe.

Meantime, Evan finally called me that Monday, the day after my last blog entry. He was checking to see how I was, which actually surprised me. He had called again in the middle of the night over the weekend, and I didn't answer fast enough, so I left him a rather chilly message that Sunday that if he actually wanted to talk to me, he might try calling me at 2:00 p.m. rather than 2:00 a.m., because I *sleep!* So, he did: at 2:00 p.m.

I told him I was very disappointed that he didn't come to see me in the hospital or even at home while I recovered. He said his life pretty much got turned upside down. He lost his apartment and was officially couch surfing. Fuck. I couldn't even imagine. He put some stuff in storage and got rid of the rest of it, he said.

I didn't know what to say—get a job? But I knew from personal experience that's easier said than done. Still, he was young and good looking, and I couldn't imagine that he couldn't tend bar or something.

I asked about his family. He said they didn't care. His sister had gotten a better job, traveled a lot, and didn't even offer her place to him while she was gone, he said. I wondered if it had dawned on him that maybe it was because he gave nothing in return to everyone who did so much for him—including me.

But, the good heart that I have, I told him if he was in a bind, he could crash here. I also made it clear that I was still in physical repair and couldn't have sex—not that I wouldn't like to.

What was this hold he had on me? Why did I care? I was seeing a new therapist the next day. Maybe she could figure it out.

I would see Dr. Isik the next week after I got back from Whidbey. I hoped he could give me an idea of when the next step would be—which was the symmetry part: where he would lift my right breast to match the new one.

CHAPTER 32

IS IT POSSIBLE THAT GOOD THINGS COULD BE COMING?

Blog post: Monday, September 3, 2012
I Think the Universe Is Opening up for Me

The past week has been sort of extraordinary. I went to Whidbey Island the twenty-sixth through the twenty-eighth of August, and although I didn't see any cheap real estate that I loved (or groovy job opportunities), I may have stumbled onto something completely unexpected.

I met this very nice lady who was going through a program right now to get her MFA in creative writing. As it turned out, I know someone else who just graduated from the same program. It's quite interesting, fully accredited, and is offered through the Northwest Academy of Literary Arts. You spend two nine-day stints on the island at the lovely Capt. Whidbey Inn and do the rest online. My friend who just graduated and this woman both raved about it. It's just for creative writers—and there's absolutely no math involved! So, I'm contemplating applying.

Meantime, all sorts of interesting opportunities are coming my way. Nothing has solidified yet, but I do have one for-sure interview this week for a job that is related to another field I've been interested in, but I haven't pursued it before, because it would involve eventually opening my own business. But if I got this job, I'd get a taste of the industry— ditto for one other opportunity. I don't want to say too much more, in case none of it works out.

Meantime, my old boss, Mary, called me. She's such a dear: always looking out for me. Next Sunday, the Susan Komen Foundation is having a hosted luncheon for breast cancer survivors on the Holland America Cruise ship, the Oosterdam, while it's at the cruise terminal. They want me to go, as a survivor, and to also write a story about it for the "Pink Pages," which they do for breast cancer awareness month (October). So of course, I said yes! I can't wait to see what one of these big-ass cruise ships looks like.

But there's more to this one too. One of the executive VPs with Holland America is on the Mercer Island City Council, and Mary has access to him. And they're hiring. So, she's going to try to arrange a meeting for me. I've applied with them before (PR-type jobs), but they ignore me. I am telling you, it's connections that get you a job anymore. I paid forty dollars to one of those head hunter websites, and they either send me jobs that I know I don't qualify for, or some dingbat calls me and wants me to enter the exciting world of insurance sales. No thanks, I did my time with commission sales. I couldn't deal with that stress again.

I continue to get better and better. I saw Dr. Isik (the plastic surgeon) Wednesday, and he is ever impressed with my progress. I have a lot of swelling still over the new breast, and he said it's called fat necrosis. It really bugs me: it feels like I have a lot of pressure on my chest and like I've got something under my arm all the time when it's down. But he said it will go down and settle into one little spot, and then he'll pluck it out. So, I see him again in three weeks.

Then on Friday, I had my next-to-the-last Herceptin infusion! Yay! Then I can finally get my port out. I've had it in since March of 2011, and I'm really sick of it. Dr. Isik may take it out rather than my surgical oncologist, since he's still got work to do on me. There will be another *procedure to lift the right breast and get them both to match once the swelling is down.*

I can't believe I'm almost done with Herceptin. My heart is doing well; in fact, they scheduled me for an echocardiogram the tenth. But I just saw a new study come out that said women who have undergone chemo for breast cancer and then used Herceptin are at greater risk for heart disease—super. But I'm not too worried, because my heart has been stalwart so far. It's a good ticker, thank God. I credit that to exercise.

I start restorative yoga next weekend and Tango lessons September 11 for six weeks—which should be fun. I'm not ready for Pilates again because of the abdominal incision, but I'll get there.

But Abbey and I are walking the woods again in Lincoln Park, and it's been great.

The only downer is my car. After I left the cancer institute Friday, my car would not unlock. The keyless entry hasn't worked for some time, but this time, even the key didn't work manually. I called two locksmiths, but they both said BMWs are too secure, and they can't get into them. So, I had to be towed to the dealer. I got there ten minutes before they closed. They were kind enough to give me a really, really nice loaner (a 2010 328I), but it's going to cost about a grand to get into my car again. Shit. They had to order the new tumbler assembly, so it could be I won't get my car back until Friday. But being the dealership, they took it upon themselves to comb through the whole car and rattle off this laundry list of stuff I had better get fixed at outrageous cost, and I told the service advisor, forget it—just get me in the damn car.

I have a wonderful mechanic with a little shop right here in West Seattle, and I'm going to have him look at all these so-called repairs I need, and if he says it's all BS, then fine; if it's not B.S., then I'm going to start shopping for a new car, because I just won't put any more money into this one. It's been a fabulous car; I've loved it, and I feel very safe in it. But I just hate repair after repair. I need a dependable car. I just hate the bus: too many weirdos.

So for now, I'm not ready to leave the city. I still like it here: the culture, the restaurants, and I have to say, the weather! No kidding—we're on day forty-three (I think) of no rain! If we make it another week, it will be a record! Of course, the rain will return—it's Seattle!—but like my cousin Sheila says, "At least you don't have to shovel rain."

Seattle hasn't experienced the horrible drought or the horrible storms like they get in the gulf coast. Really, it's pretty mild here. The gloom gets tough in the winter, but at least it's not dark like Alaska gets in the dead of winter. Things could be worse.

Hmm…my love life got interesting this weekend too. Well, first—no shocker—I sent Evan a text to see how he was doing and if he was okay. He didn't answer, so I went to bed. Then, he called me at some ungodly hour (three or four in the morning) and needed a place to crash. I could hear really loud people in the background, and he was obviously partying, as usual. I told him he didn't dare bring a bunch of people over here.

They, whoever they were, dumped him off at the nearby gas station, and he walked here, gently knocking on my door. He really looked awful. He was drunk and disheveled. I let him into my bed, and he seduced me, of course. I didn't sleep very well after that.

In the morning, I was up, read most of the paper, had coffee, and talked to the BMW guy about my car. Then I heard Evan calling me to the bedroom. He knew I was totally pissed about the car. We talked, made love again, and then I had to get rolling, because I was going to a Mariner's Game. He needed a haircut.

I took him as far as I was going—to the stadium—and from there, he was going to walk to some friend's place on Capitol Hill, where he had a two-night invitation to crash.

He was seriously wearing on me. I cared deeply for him, and I didn't want him to be out in the cold, but he needed to get some ambition going and quit chasing a dream.

He was thirty-five! My God, did he realize he'd be forty in five years? Time goes faster as you get older.

I didn't tell him, because it's none of his business, but I had a date scheduled for Sunday morning. This was yet another new guy off the dating website, so I didn't have much hope, but he seemed funny and looked cute.

He was both—and more. And we hit it off. What's more, he too is a cancer survivor. He had lymphoma—scary, scary. He still had a tumor in his chest, but he said it was not a big deal. He also still had a port (he had said, "I'll show you my port if you show me yours"—it was funny). But the thing was—he got it!

His name was Bob. Bob had his treatment at Swedish too. We had different medical oncologists but had the same radiation guy. It was a trip. He had a full head of hair too. I don't know if he lost it during chemo; I didn't ask.

Bob would be forty-four that month, so I was twelve years older, but as you, dear reader, have figured out, I like younger men—and he liked older women. We talked for two hours over coffee and looking out over the water on Alki Beach. I really liked him. I felt a connection.

He had a good job (refreshing), and twelve acres near Port Townsend. He was heading over there for five days to knock down the weeds and clean up the grounds. He said he had a fifth-wheel with running water and everything on it. That's where he went to escape.

He also had family here. His mom and step-dad were in Edmonds, and he had a techie brother in the area. He had never married or had kids, but he'd had several long-term relationships. That always concerns me, but gads, after all the crap I've gone through, it was just nice to talk to someone who "gets it."

I asked if he wanted to see me again, and he said he would. I was happy about that. He gave me a very gentle kiss on the lips, and we parted ways. He had to work before he left for his property.

I had hoped he'd call. But he never did.

CHAPTER 33

EVAN IN CRISIS

In the middle of the night, on a Friday, I got a text from Evan. It simply said "Bitch." At first I couldn't read it, so I put my glasses on and was shocked. What? I said, "Why are you calling me that?" He replied, "I'm tired, in a hotel room—what else do I have."

I told him to go to sleep: that he'd feel better in the morning. I still didn't understand why he called me a bitch, as I'd done nothing but be kind to him. His response was, "All women are evil."

I told him I was ending this discussion. "I am not evil. Goodnight."

He responded with bitch, again.

I said, "You break my heart. I've done nothing to deserve this. What is the matter with you? Do you think you're the only one who is suffering? Think about it and all of the physical and mental pain I've been through the past two years. Pull yourself up by the bootstraps, get a haircut, and get a job. Help other people. and your life will turn around."

His response was that I am a square, but "I still love you."

I told him: I'm not a square and don't call people names! "I have feelings. You are being so incredibly mean."

I was so upset, crying half of the day, that I decided to reach out to his family to find out what was going on. Evan was the oldest of five children, and I found his little brother first on Facebook, so I sent him a message. He was the wrong one to reach out to. Oh, he felt bad for the way I was treated, and he was kind to me, but he clearly is a really, really right-wing Christian nut-job.

"This is what has happened to Evan," he said. "Satan fooled him into thinking he could find peace, happiness, and joy apart from Christ way back when he was in high school, and what you see in him right now is simply the end result of a consistent, never-ending pattern of hardening his heart against what he knows to be true. He has become a druggie for no other reason than to block out the pain he has caused and silence his conscience. Where my parents failed is they didn't ensure we children understood that even though mom and dad were Christians, that didn't mean we were Christians. That creates the perfect storm, because children then receive all the benefits (the love, the closeness, the blessings) of Christianity without having to make any sacrifice."

Okay, Evan has told me about his Christian upbringing, and it sounded pretty severe, but still, I thought his brother was being a bit judgmental, especially when he went on to say that "it's too late" for Evan—some support. But he did give me Evan's sister's phone number; fortunately, she lives in Seattle too. I met her at Evan's birthday party and found her to be quite together and charming.

I tried to call her, and then I sent a text. I told her I was concerned about his recent behavior. She was actually in Arizona on business, but she sent me a long message saying that he'd been acting pretty bizarre for a while, and that he had been in and out of the hospital for some time. I did not know that, nor did I understand. She said he had distanced himself from the family and had been pretty mean to them in general and didn't want their help unless it was for money. She also said I was not the first person to come to the family in the last year.

"We love him and are concerned, but until he wants help, there's not much we can do," she said. "Glad he has good friends like you."

As it turned out, he'd been in and out of the hospital numerous times for threatening suicide. His sister got back to town, and I waited for three days to hear from her to see about getting together so she could explain to me what the problem was. By that time, Evan was in the hospital again, and this time was different. When I finally got to speak with her in person the next day, she said this time he had sent a message to a friend—that was basically a suicide note and a plan on how he was going to do it. The friend called the police; they picked him up and took him to the hospital.

Their father flew in that day from Arizona. His sister said the dad was frantically trying to come up with a plan, and he did. An aunt and an uncle with a large business in another state could set him up in a place and a job. She said he was receptive at first, but by the next day, the day I met with her, Evan was back to his old defiant self, accusing them of judging him. He refused to see his dad again—which really hurt his dad's feelings—so his dad flew home.

Apparently, he got out of the hospital the next day. He told his sister he had a place to live for two weeks. But then what—back on the street?

I asked her if maybe he was bi-polar. They didn't know. He refused to get deep enough therapy to find out. Both she and I acknowledged that he smoked way too much pot, and it was draining him of his ambition. She said his downhill slide began about three years ago when he lost his last real job. I had met him about six months later, but he didn't have a mean bone in his body then.

I was very depressed over this. I prayed for him. I didn't want people to judge me, either, because I still loved him even after all the shit he'd put me through. There was a good person in there, I knew it.

I left him a phone message the day he got out of the hospital. I just said I wasn't mad at him, and I was here for support as one human being to another, and that I loved him.

I didn't hear from him—which was no surprise.

His sister had said to me that she knew he cared about me and would regret whatever he had said once he got through all of this. He was probably already embarrassed about what he said.

But I worried: was he going to end up dead either by his own hand or by getting beat up on the streets before he woke up?

The few friends I talked to about this told me to be careful: to take care of myself and not get too stressed out about this. But it was hard to not worry about someone you loved when they were on the abyss.

They were right though. My back was hurting like a son-of-a-bitch, and my boob was still sore. I still had so much pain to recover from physically, and I needed to protect myself emotionally.

Blog post: Thursday, September 20, 2012
The End Is Near

As I sit in the treatment chair, right now, I'm getting my last Herceptin infusion. I never thought this day would come. I'm also getting a flu shot, as I do every year, but I am even more vigilant because of my white blood count still being low. It's weird; it was 2.3 today. Three weeks ago it was at three. In the four-range is normal. It takes forever for all of the chemo effects to wear off.

I have a new problem, and I hope it's not serious. My back has been bothering me a great deal. This started way before cancer. It's where disc L5 joins the SI and is most prevalent on the right side. There have been a few incidents recently where I thought it was going to go out on me. It hurts terribly. So, next Tuesday, I'm having a bone scan and MRI to see what's up with that. I got sort of scared. Bone cancer, of course, shot through my head, but Dr. Kaplan said that's an odd place to get it. Hopefully, it's just pressure on the disc or something.

But I'm thrilled to say, the reconstruction mess is getting much better. I saw Dr. Isik yesterday, and he's ready for the next step. So next Thursday, I'll have another little surgery—this time in the OR in his office. This is to remove the fat necrosis over my new left breast and lift the right side so I am symmetrical. I was really surprised that he thought I was ready. Since he's already going to have me down for the count (under anesthesia), he will remove this damn port that's been in me since March 2011! For that, I am super stoked.

There will still be a few more little things to do, but I'm beginning to see light at the end of the tunnel.

Fear of cancer coming back will always live with me, however.

There's still no job, but two people are leaving the Bellevue office of the company I worked for. One is leaving for a job with a business journal; the other is having a baby. So, I applied—it's not like they don't know me. So, I'm going to visit with Craig, the editor, on Monday. It's certainly not like they don't know my work. I'm to the point now where I just want to get back to work.

I'm also psyched, because there is a new condo on the market—that is even better than the one I was close to making an offer on before I was laid off in March. This one is in a building with only five units; I actually had looked at another one in the same building, but she wanted too much money, I thought, and it did not have a covered parking place. I saw this in Sunday's paper and thought I'd go check it out (it was an open house). I figured it was the one I looked at before—but no! It's the one above it, so it has vaulted ceilings—which makes it feel much bigger—and it has a covered parking space.

Not only that, it's an estate sale, so the son of whoever died put in an all-new kitchen: cabinets, flooring, counters, and stainless steel appliances! It also has new paint and nice new carpet—all this and a view of Puget Sound and the Olympic Mountains. So if I get re-hired, I'm going to give it a shot. I will feel much better in a better neighborhood and lovely place.

I have been sort of down due to concerns about other people in my life who are having even greater struggles. It just seems like there's so much bad ju-ju going on. I hope things turn around for all of us very soon.

CHAPTER 34

GOT MY JOB BACK!

My interview with the editor in Bellevue went very well. By Wednesday of that week, I was getting nervous though, because I hadn't heard a peep.

Thursday morning, I went through the whole routine of getting ready for surgery for my nip/tuck on my breasts. I was waiting for Ben, who was sweet enough to give me a ride and pick me up from that one, and my phone rang at 9:25 a.m. It was Craig—would I like the job?

Of course, I said yes. I would start Wednesday, October 3. I wanted at least five days to recover from this little surgery, and I was so glad I planned that, because this hurt way more than I thought it would too: ouch—big time.

My right breast, which was lifted, was totally bruised: every color of the rainbow. And it itched—which was driving me nuts. The new boob really hurt, because he ended up doing quite a bit more augmentation than he planned. Then they had to do some fat grafting to fill in a divot in my upper chest. So, yes, I hurt. From the waist up I looked like a war zone. Oh, how attractive it was.

Craig's call came at an awkward moment because I had to leave at 9:30 for the doctor's office. He said HR needed some stuff, and typically they want it the same day, but when I told him I was out the door for surgery, he said the next day would be fine.

I would be in the Bellevue office, not my sweet Mercer Island office, reporting on Issaquah. Fine. I was so sick of looking for work it was nauseating.

It was so nice of Ben to give me the rides. I had no one else to ask, because Jim was out of town, and Mira had just started a new job. Ben had tons of seniority and could work remotely, so it wasn't an issue. He's a good soul. The timing of our relationship was just awful. I'm so glad we are friends, even though I don't see him often.

Meantime, there was not a peep from Evan. His sister hadn't heard anything either. I would just pray he was alive. My new therapist wisely told me that I couldn't stress over him right then though. I had to get well, concentrate on the job, and take care of myself.

She saw a pattern of me taking abuse (from men) and I needed to set up boundaries and stick to them: no more Linda taking anymore crap from people who put me down and made me feel bad about myself.

That said, even with sore boobs, I made an offer on the condo! I was so excited—if I got it, I'd move over Thanksgiving. It would be so good for my soul to have that view and the light—not to mention a much better "hood" where I would feel safer. I was on pins and needles waiting to hear on my offer.

And, as part of my "demands" for going back to the old company, I told Craig I planned to drive over to Idaho October 11 (my fifty-sixth birthday—I still can't believe I'm that old!) to see Taylor, whose birthday was October 13, and my pals over there for a long weekend, and that was fine. I figured I wouldn't get any time off for a long, long time, and with a potential move coming up, I'd better go then. I looked forward to seeing my peeps over there!

Blog post: Sunday, October 21, 2012
I Need More Hours in a Day

So much has happened in the past month I don't even believe it. I'm back to work as of October 3, and I am in the process of buying the wonderful condo I talked about in my last blog. But I'm so damn tired all the time. It makes me angry with myself that I can't keep up the pace. I even woke myself up this morning, because I was snoring! I never snored before.

Going back to work has been a real adjustment. I wasn't used to getting up and having to pretty much step on the gas right away.

Combined with working through the condo transaction, I barely have time for all the things I was taking for granted: like nice walks with Abbey or practicing my ukulele.

I'm still not my old self. September 27, I had the little nip and tuck I mentioned before. This included lifting the right breast. Dammit, everything hurts worse than I think it's going to! I had a follow-up October 10, the day before my birthday, and Dr. Isik said it looked good, but I still have so much swelling on the new breast. He prescribed me some antibiotics, which helped, but I still feel like a freak, because they don't match.

Then, the words I never thought I'd hear in my whole life: November 6 is nipple day! Oh yay—but that will be the end of surgeries. So, since I had a skin-sparing mastectomy, I've got enough tissue there for him to push it together and make a new nipple. A few weeks after that comes the tattoo of the areola.

But I'm tired and bummed, because I'm not exercising as much as I'd like to, because I'm so tired. Hopefully things will settle down one of these days. I'm going to have to hire movers when I move into the condo, because it's on the third floor, and I can't lift much these days. Which brings me to my back: no, I don't have bone cancer, thank God. But I do have arthritis in my back now, and my L5/S1 are a bit worn out, but this doesn't require surgery—which I wouldn't do anyway: No more cutting on me!

I went to a rehabilitative doc, and he said given my history of Pilates, to get back into it, and it will strengthen my back again. I know it will. I've just been too tired to do it. He was a cool guy.

That said, I did get Abbey to the park today for our usual hike, and I did fine. Tonight, I'm going to a ball. You heard right: a ball, as in Cinderella went to the ball!—although, I don't feel like Cinderella.

Mira talked me into this a long time ago. It's called "An Evening in Vienna," and this year, it's at the University of Washington in their huge ballroom that's apparently very beautiful and newly remodeled. It's black tie, so I had to buy a dress: a gown, if you will. I got a good deal on a very flattering, long black "mermaid" dress. It's ruched through the bodice, so it's very figure-flattering. It has a higher neckline, but it is sheer on top, so it hides all my scars that might otherwise be revealed. I'm so self-conscious.

Friday night, Mira and I went to a three-hour ball prep, which focused on brushing up on waltz and foxtrot, with a little bit of polka, which may sound dorky, but it was the most fun. It's like how they danced in Gone with the Wind. Waltz was considered far too scandalous then because of the closeness with your dance partner! Ha-ha! Anyway, God I hope there are some decent leads (guys) there tonight, because I was stepped on more than once and even have a bruise on my left big toe. A follow is only as good as her lead, and if they push you down the dance floor or invade your dance space, it's a drag.

But, I guess it's good I'm getting out among them! I was too tired to even go to a movie last night after my day of chores and errands.

I did go over to my old stomping grounds for my birthday and Taylor's birthday. I drove over on my birthday and came home Sunday. He is living with a couple of guys now, and it's a typical bachelor pad, but it looked fine. I saw a lot of my old pals, but again, it was too short and fast. It's good to go over there, but I really don't miss the place—just the people.

I think I'm going to get back into the condo Tuesday and hopefully get a couple of contractors in to bid on a new hot water heater and possibly new tile around the tub. Everything else is pretty much done, but the seller's representative re-tiled the bathroom floor with nice new big tiles, but the tub still has the original old icky white tile around it with a black accent, so it looks weird. I want shit done before I move in.

One more thing: I had applied for an MFA program in creative writing, but I didn't get in. I was very disappointed, but as my friend Taryn has said, and I believe this: God opens the doors that are meant to open and closes the other ones. It would probably kill me to add school on top of all of this other stuff right now.

So, if all goes well, I'll be in the condo at the end of November. If I don't do Christmas cards this year, don't freak. I can only do so much.

It's time to put the pretty on. Hopefully no one will step on me!

CHAPTER 35

MOVING IN AND SETTLING DOWN

Blog post: Sunday, November 11, 2012
Something Huge to Look Forward To!

Wow! I might get to close on the condo this week! Words cannot describe how excited I am about moving to my "deluxe apartment in the sky," (which is only on the third floor, but I am on top and I have a view of Puget Sound and the Olympic Mountains). George Jefferson would be proud!

I don't plan to move in until the end of the month, but I want time to clean (my way), and Nina, my contractor friend, needs time to get the bathroom done.

I decided to re-tile around the bath enclosure. It's the original tile, and not only is it ugly and doesn't match the new floor the seller put in, the grout is pitted, so ten to one it's wet behind the tile. So, this will be mass destruction in the bathroom. I picked out killer tile (with a glass tile accent), which Nina will also put around the sink backsplash to pull it all together. The glass tile has a little bit of mother-of-pearl in it for some bling, and then I saw a shower curtain with little crystals in it—for a little more bling! I have to buy a mirror for the bathroom, too, because there isn't one, so I'm hoping to find something sort of vintage. And I'll get new towels! I am so excited to be able to get some of my personality into a place!

I'm also having Nina put in a new hot water heater. The one there now works, but it's older than dirt, and I would just freak if it leaked on the new carpet. And it's in the master bedroom closet, so if it leaked, it would destroy my shoes and leak on everyone below me—none of it good.

To think, just a year ago I was still in a chemo haze and bald. I had a trim yesterday—my hair is just insane: it's so thick and curly! It's really looking cool now. I donated my wig and my breast prosthetics to the American Cancer Society, and they were thrilled! It made me feel good, too, not only to get rid of those things, but knowing there are women out there who don't even have insurance to get them, so hopefully, someone will use these and feel better about the whole ugly situation.

On election day, it was also "get-a-nipple day." It didn't hurt, but I have more fat necrosis over the new boob, and it does hurt. But I have to be sedated for him to do that, and I'm just too busy right now to take time to be knocked out again. So, it's scheduled for December 13. I asked Dr. Isik if this is going to be a constantly re-occurring thing, and he said this should be the last time. But it really does hurt. It feels like my boob is going to explode. Once it settles down, then he will tattoo the areola, and I'm done! If I still can't handle the mastectomy/reconstruction scars, I have saved a newspaper article for a year now about a female tattoo artist here in Seattle who specializes in art over those scars—maybe some vines, John Lennon, or Eddie Vedder? Who knows!

I still haven't gone back to Pilates—simply because of time. When I'm not working, I'm dealing with planning this move. I've packed maybe fifteen boxes and have been purging crap I don't want or need anymore. And work has been busy! Being the only reporter covering Issaquah, believe it or not, is hard! There's a lot going on over there: mainly with growth issues. Then I covered two local political races, one which was nasty. God, I'm glad the election is over. And I am so relieved that Obama was re-elected. I wasn't ready for my vagina to be sewn shut!

I'm still trying to have a little bit of a life. I did go to the ball with Mira, and it was fun—even though I only danced about five times. But it was cool to see people dressed up in flannel Seattle! Almost all the women had on long gowns (some vintage), and all of the gentlemen had on tuxes, except one dude in a suit, and two in kilts—go figure.

Last night, I went to the Broadway play Wicked *at the Paramount Theater. It was fabulous! What a great story! It's about the witches of Oz way before Dorothy drops in. The two gals in the lead roles of Glinda and Elphaba were absolutely amazing. There are some seriously talented stage actors out there. They both had such unreal, powerful voices. There were flying monkeys, the Wizard…it was very cool.*

After packing boxes for a while today, I had a coffee date with a nice man I met online. I've gone on several of these coffee dates that have gone absolutely nowhere, but this was different. There was a connection. He's my age. (Imagine that: me, possibly interested in someone my own age! Ha-ha!)

We'll see where it goes. He's lived here all his life—beautiful Paul Newman blue eyes.

I'm going to Mira's for Thanksgiving, since my kitchen might be in two places, and I have no one coming anyway. Taylor normally spends Thanksgiving with his dad, because they like to go hunting. Then, he'll come here for Christmas. He's looking forward to seeing the new place. He really likes it down there (Alki-Beach area) too.

So, if I can just make it through this move without falling apart, I'll be good!

Blog post: Monday, December 3, 2012
I Love My New Home—But Not My One Neighbor

I'm so tired and worn out: physically and mentally. My eyes are bloodshot, and my back and boob hurt. However, I am in my new home (slept here four nights now), and it's so much nicer! Even though the weather has been horrible the past week, the view is still amazing. Watching Puget Sound with white caps is pretty awesome. I am sleeping a little better, because it's quieter, and the building is so much better insulated, I don't freeze. At the apartment, it was like there was nothing in the walls, so then I'd crank the heat up and get too hot.

Moving is so hard. I've decided this is it. I'll die in this place! It's been challenging trying to figure out where to put stuff. I have more storage, but I am quite sure the living room is smaller, so furniture placement has been a bitch. Now I'm trying to figure out where to put a Christmas tree!

The only negative has been the weirdo woman directly below me. I'll call her Kim (not her real name—I'm afraid she'd sue me). Apparently everyone in the building has experienced the wrath of Kim. My God, there are only five units, but I think she is determined to make life hell for the other four homeowners.

I couldn't get my beautiful pink bike into my storage locker, as it's too long (many of you have seen it: a pink cruiser with a basket that Abbey will ride in). So, I talked to Chuck and Tessa, my wonderful neighbors across the hall, who are the treasurer and secretary of the association, respectively. They suggested I park it in the lobby, since it's so cute. The lobby is secure, and there is only one unit on the ground floor, and the owner spends most of her time in Hawaii, so she is rarely there. She doesn't care either.

Then, the first curt e-mail came from Kim. She wanted me to remove my bike, because it's common area, and it doesn't belong there. I responded that I really didn't have anywhere else to put it, and that I was a recent cancer survivor and didn't have it in me to carry it up three flights of stairs. I also pointed out that Chuck, Tessa, the lady in Hawaii, and I are all okay with it, so the majority didn't mind.

Then on Saturday, Kim sends me an e-mail, (mind you, I'm right upstairs) to let me know that to "help" me out, she put my bike into the storage area. I flipped. She set it in the middle so no one else would be able to get into their storage lockers and where it could get all scratched up. That bike was the last really cool gift from Mom and Pop before they died. They bought it for me after I graduated from college in 2005. (Yes, I'm a late bloomer). So, it has special meaning to me too.

Kim says in her e-mail that Chuck is "not in charge of managing the building."

I was livid, so with the help of my new friend, Daniel, we moved it back into the lobby. I e-mailed Chuck, Tessa, and the gal in Hawaii of the latest developments. Chuck sent Kim a message, which he copied to everyone, saying she's right, he's not the building manager but neither is she, and he said, "If you do not specify a CC&R or by-law, your commands and threatening language carry no weight." I had e-mailed Kim, pleading with her not to touch my bike again—that it is neither ugly nor in the way. I also mentioned my donation of a much better rug for the entrance to the building: a real nice storm chaser rug from LLBean.

So, this was yesterday. I go out to recycle some more boxes and paper as I'm unloading, and my bike is gone from the lobby—again. That bitch shoved it back into the storage unit. This time, I hauled it out, put it back in the lobby, and left a note on her door (since she didn't answer when I knocked loudly—and I know she's in there) that if she touched my bike again, I'd call the cops.

I had barely put the note up when she's at my door pounding. I opened the door, and our first meeting began as a shouting match. She's crazy. She is trying to sell her unit—I looked at it over a year ago! It's overpriced and smells of her old dog. She's convinced that my bike in the lobby will deter potential buyers for her unit. Really—how about dropping the price and change out the carpet?

Kim went on about how we're all rule breakers and how awful Chuck is. I shut her right down. Chuck and Tessa are a lovely couple: they even sent me a gorgeous Christmas floral arrangement as a welcome gift. She was just screaming at me: how she was going to get a lawyer and call 911; it was horrible. I asked her why she couldn't just be neighborly. She said I wasn't being a good neighbor, etc., and then she crossed herself (like Catholics do). I looked at her and asked her why she was crossing herself—did she think I was Satan? Her eyes got huge, and she said, "Oh, you're not a very nice person." I felt like saying, "And you are a bitter, nasty woman."

At one point, she said to me, "Well, honey, I'm dying." I asked her what was wrong with her, and she said it was none of my business.

To make a horrid story short, we both finally calmed down and came up with a possible solution. The fifth owner, Catherine, is in Florida until December 15. Kim said her storage locker is empty. If Catherine will let me put my bike in her storage locker: great; if not—get this— Kim says she'll take all of her stuff out of hers, and we can put it in there. I said, "Are you kidding; it means that much to you?"

She said it did. She's absolutely nuts. I truly pray to God she sells. Every single person in here has been attacked by her on some issue. She said she's selling, because the building has changed with all of us "new people" who don't follow the rules. When she finally got out of my face, I was shaking and crying. I had to take half a Xanax and drink some wine to calm down.

So, other than that (!), it's all good. My bathroom turned out beautiful: I got new towels, shower curtain, and rug, and with the gorgeous new tile, it looks pretty. Abbey seems to like the place. She likes looking out the big window at the world below.

Also, I've had four dates now with Daniel, who I guess I shall refer to as my new beau. He's so sweet. I saw his home briefly Saturday night, and I was in awe of the Beatles memorabilia he has—he's like me! We have some of the same Beatles posters. He also owns eight beautiful guitars: nice ones—Fender, etc. His home is in the Mt. Baker neighborhood, a very nice area near Lake Washington on the west side. He is into classic sports cars and music, and he has a Harley-Davidson, which I can't wait to ride on when the weather gets better.

I called him, crying, after the whole run in with Kim. I was so upset. I hope I didn't scare him off! He helped me with a few honey-dos around the condo too.

And I am so grateful to Nina for the fine job she did on everything for me. She's a wonderful person and very competent contractor. If you're in Seattle, look her up: Velvet Hammer.

So, more unpacking and getting a Christmas tree up are on the agenda this week in addition to work. Colleen is flying in Saturday night for a short business trip, so I'm going to have her help me hang art, since she's got the interior designer eye going on.

She flies out the thirteenth, the day I have the remaining fat necrosis removed from my boob. It's a short surgery, but I will be IV-sedated. Daniel will take me and drive me home. He's such a sweetie.

I was supposed to have a massage yesterday, but I rescheduled for Friday. I was just too frazzled. So, I have that to look forward to, along with Col coming, Daniel, and then, of course, my baby Taylor coming for Christmas.

If you're on my Christmas card list and don't get one this year, it's because it's just too much right now. I've never missed a beat on this, but I need to allow myself to let it go if I get too stressed out. That doesn't mean I love any of you less.

CHAPTER 36

MY HAPPY HOME

I've not blogged since December 3, and now it's a new year: 2013.

I had the procedure to remove fat necrosis on December 13, and I've had one checkup since, requiring antibiotics again, but I should be okay now. I had the areola tattoo—it looks funny right now because it's darker, but Dr. Isik said it will fade. It didn't hurt getting it, but I was a bit sore for the following week.

So the journey ends, I guess, except for ongoing monitoring of my blood and mammograms for the next five years.

I love my condo. The job is going okay. I broke a story the *Seattle Times* and KIRO News Radio picked up, so that made me feel good. Everything has been so confusing for the past two years. Honestly, I'm so glad I've written this memoir, because otherwise I wouldn't remember any of this.

Christmas was just okay. I felt under so much pressure to get settled, decorate, cook and clean. My time with my son was not great, but that's another story.

I brought in this new year with Daniel at his family's cabin—just the two of us. It was really nice and not too far out of town. It's on a little lake about an hour north, so it was peaceful.

But, as it seems to go sometimes, there really is not a "happy ever after." Daniel dumped me quite unceremoniously after three awesome months together. I truly don't get it. He said he loved me, but he wasn't "in love" with me, and it's over. Fuck me. No wait…fuck him.

He's got baggage, but don't we all at this age? He just couldn't seem to handle too much stimulation at once, I think.

He has a very troubled son who has "made his life hell for the past ten years," he says. Well, I knew that. The son has mental illness and gets in trouble or ends up on the street. He's thirty. So he tried to put it on the son: that he couldn't handle a relationship and his son at the same time. His first suggestion was that we take a break.

My heart hurt so badly. But then I got to thinking, "You know, dude, I went through cancer pretty much by myself—except when one of my girls would come and take care of me—and if you can't accept something positive in your life, then you need therapy." I sent him an e-mail to that effect and also left a voice message.

Finally, two days later he called with the "I'm-not-in-love-with-you" stuff, and I fell apart.

I cried for two solid days.

But I'm okay. He probably did me a favor. He wasn't very adventurous. He didn't seem to want to try anything new or travel. I've picked myself up and dusted myself off. I have a big personality, I guess, and these unadventurous, stuck-in-their-rut-way-of-life guys just can't handle it—fine.

I plan to enjoy whatever is left of my life

As far as Evan goes, he's working again and was back in his old apartment building with a roommate, but then he decided to move to Spokane. He sounds so much better: grounded again. I will miss him, but perhaps the change in scenery was what he needed to find peace with himself. So, I can see him when I go over there to see my old peeps.

He did come and see my new place before he left. I cooked dinner...we made love—the usual. I can't help the fact that I'm still very attracted to him. We have amazing chemistry, but he's not good for my heart. I will always care about Evan, but I don't really want to grow old alone. Who knows: maybe he'll grow up someday. I doubt it; he's far too self-absorbed. At least I know what to expect with him, and we remain friends. But I am ever hopeful that he'll come around and realize one day how much he means to me, and perhaps we can grow old together.

But I've learned, as the Stones once sang, that "I Have no Expectations." Relationships are difficult. I don't want an unhappy one ever, ever again. But it is nice to have a shoulder to cry on or someone to hold my hand, but it is what it is sometimes. I must say, I think the men in Seattle are fairly lame. It seems they can't talk to women unless it's through social media. Techie chicken shits, afraid of any sort of commitment.

I'm so glad I love my new place, because it grounds me. I've taken care of myself now for a long time, and I will continue to do so. I did yoga for a while, and now I'm doing what's called Lagree Fitness, which combines Pilates with strength training. It's really hard for me, because I am still sore in so many places and not as strong as I used to be, but I am determined to get my power back—in many ways. I've also gone skiing and plan to go a few more times. It felt awesome! I did seven runs at Stevens Pass, and I hadn't skied in a year.

I do know I want to live—and I don't mean just be alive with blood flowing through my veins.

I want to go glamping; I'm planning to go back to Europe next summer with Colleen; and I want to laugh a lot and embrace all my wonderful friends. Because for all I know, the cancer could come back. The way I feel now is that I don't know if I have another fight left in me.

I am not terribly afraid of death. I have faith that if the cancer takes me, I'll be with God, and I'll be all right.

And I'll be jamming.

EPILOGUE

I ran in my first Susan G. Komen Race for the Cure, June 2, 2013. It was a truly inspiring event to be a part of. Seattle Center was a sea of pink — 9,000 people participated! I got there a little after 7 a.m. which was not easy, but I had time to check in my bag, use the restroom and go up to the Survivor's area at the top of Fischer Pavilion and I did indeed get a shiny gold cape for raising over $500.

Everyone, especially the volunteers, were so wonderful. They treated us like we were really special, yet we were just part of a very large group of people in the same club – a club we really did not choose to be a part of.

I had my picture taken in my cape, which was over my pink Survivor's shirt. I also had on my gold ribbon necklace that Col gave me, and I received a gold dog tag, again for the fundraising. Later I would have my beautiful medal for finishing and pink beads hanging around my neck. It was so much fun!

My knee hurt later, and I was tired, but I felt good. It was weird. When I crossed the finish line I started to cry because people were clapping and cheering and it just seemed so unreal. This lady made eye contact with me — I don't know who she was — and I just gravitated to her and she hugged me and let me cry on her shoulder for a minute. It was profound.

There was a fabulous band, so I danced on the lawn, had a chair massage and participated in the Survivor's march, which made me cry again.

I don't know what's going on, but breast cancer is back on everyone's radar again. The very beautiful and famous actress Angelina Jolie recently announced that she had a preventative double mastectomy: and reconstruction, because she carried a mutation of the BRCA1 gene. That's what killed my friend from my first support group.

I thought that was very gutsy, and it did make me feel weak that I didn't have the nerve to have the mastectomy from the get go. Oh well, I made my decisions, and it's over.

The other profound incident was a movie I saw called "Decoding Annie Parker," which made its debut at the Seattle International Film Festival. It's about Dr. Mary-Claire King, who is a geneticist at the University of Washington, and a cancer patient, Annie Parker. King is the Dr. who figured out that BRCA1 can be inherited from either mom or dad — that there is a genetic link.

It was an amazing film. The director, Steven Bernstein, was there and spoke. It took him six years to make the movie, because he kept running out of money. It made me cry a lot, particularly the scenes of Annie in treatment and in pain. At the end of the film, the real Annie Parker and Dr. King came out and met in person for the first time. Although in the movie, they meet at the end, they did not meet until that very moment. I don't think anyone expected that. More tears.

The next night, I was covering a Relay for Life in Issaquah. Although I was on the job, the gal from the American Cancer Society asked me to participate in the survivor's lap. I did, and once again I was amazed. People clapping and cheering for us: and I'm thinking, geez all I did was get very sick. Then I realized they were happy we lived. I got another beautiful medal, and now they are both hanging from my rear view mirror.

And so it goes. Breast cancer is everywhere. A sea of pink – famous movie stars — in the movies: and I have scars to remind me. And now I have a cause I am passionate about.

I've come to terms with being alone a lot. I'm fine. I do get lonely, but I have wonderful friends who are there when I need them.

I am going to Europe in March of 2014 with Colleen. We're taking a cruise on a small riverboat (160 passengers) from Amsterdam to Basel, on the Rhine River. I cannot wait! We plan to do an added on Amsterdam two-night, three-day stay on the front end, then take a train from Basel to Paris and spend a few days in the beautiful city of lights, a city I love. I don't want to wait until I'm old to travel, because then it becomes a challenge. It's time to live, because I never know when I might die.

And the latest news is that I had a mammogram and breast MRI last month — I'm a-okay.

So, hug the woman you love tonight, whether it's your wife, mother, sister or daughter — just hug her, because this can happen to anyone, and until it goes away, you'll never hear the end of the fight to eradicate breast cancer. Save the boobs.

CPSIA information can be obtained at www.ICGtesting.com
Printed in the USA
LVOW12s0954251113

362724LV00001B/177/P